HISTORY OF MUSIC IN THE FORM OF LECTURES

HISTORY OF MUSIC IN THE FORM OF LECTURES

FREDERIC LOUIS RITTER

GYAN

Published by

Gyan Publishing House
5, Ansari Road
Daryaganj, New Delhi-110002
Phone: 011-47034999, 9811692060
E-mail: books@gyanbooks.com

Distribution Network
gyanbooks.com
India, USA, Canada, UK, Australia

ISBN: 978-93-7225-082-4 (PB)

First Published, 1870

2nd Impression 2026

Printed at: Gyan Press, Delhi.

HISTORY OF MUSIC IN THE FORM OF LECTURES
Author: FREDERIC LOUIS RITTER

HISTORY OF MUSIC,

In the Form of Lectures.

BY

FREDERIC LOUIS RITTER.

FIRST SERIES.

BOSTON:
PUBLISHED BY OLIVER DITSON & CO.,
277 WASHINGTON STREET.
NEW YORK: C. H. DITSON & CO.,
711 BROADWAY.

INTRODUCTORY.

To the young artists of America, in whose hands rests the musical future of their country, I dedicate the following pages. Our artists are entering on a new phase of existence. Our profession is no longer here, as it too long has been, at once a refuge, an exhibition platform, and a gambling bourse for ambitious amateurs, half-educated artists, unprincipled speculators, and undisciplined critics. This state of things, that generation, is passing away: humbug and puffery have lost half their power; the once pardonable weakness, that formerly excused national artistic short-comings with the plea of youth, is becoming stale and meaningless. Our musical public is beginning to have an opinion of its own. It is time that the dawn of a school of American art should appear on the horizon. And to whom shall we look for the hastening, the ripening, of this dawn, if not to our rising artists?

* * * * *

But they must arm themselves with courage, fortitude, and, above all, with honest artistic principles. For if our artists are unconvinced of the nobleness of their mission, the sanctity of their profession, the great duties which they owe to it and to themselves, with what hope shall they, as a class, expect justice and recognition from the general public? Although this will eventually be their reward, it would be worse than folly for one, passing through the furnace himself, to blind the eyes of his young colleagues to the trials they will necessarily be exposed to before they reach their goal. I do not here allude to the so often injurious influences of social *bonnes fortunes*, the flattery of family connections, the intoxication of seeing their names continually and favorably advertised, — enervating influences to which so many promising native talents have succumbed, sinking into oblivion at precisely the period of life when the mind should have attained its most harmonious and healthy development; but rather to the difficulties that beset the public career of the truly earnest artist in America. This is not the place to enlarge on the latter: I shall find opportunity hereafter to treat fully of them.

But it is absolutely necessary that I should at least allude to the Achilles heel of our present musical situation, from a social point of view especially.

* * * * *

While the state of musical culture to-day offers many elements which justify the hopes of all lovers of music; while everywhere we perceive much activity, united in many cases to promising talent,—yet music is, by many intelligent people, scarcely regarded as an art. Many persons, of tolerably liberal views, yet consider it merely as an accessory accomplishment, and would gladly banish it, if the prevailing superficial fashion (so much to be regretted) of knowing how to play, or how to sing, *a little*, were not too strong to be resisted. And many consider music as an unfit occupation for masculine minds.

None of the other arts is encumbered with so many prejudices as music. Though accessible to every human being, its right position in the family of arts is, in many cases, underrated; its philosophical and æsthetical meaning entirely overlooked, or not understood at all. About none of the other arts has so much nonsense been written, as about music. A person scarcely able to distinguish one tone or note from another, one air from another, will not hesitate to judge of, and condemn, fine musical works in a most imperative manner; nay, I have seen criticisms, novels, and sketches, on musical subjects, written by persons who could not sing or play the simplest tune, and to whom theory was a *terra incognita.*

In our day, as in earlier times, we find mankind making music the vehicle of all that is good and bad. Now it is prescribed for medical purposes; then it has to serve as a means for educating our ill-tempered youth: now it has to inspire the timid soldier with patriotic fire; then it is invoked as a helpmeet by the frivolous, &c., &c. But, worse than all, here appears an esteemed author, who does not find any thing of the sort in music, and who declares that it expresses nothing at all: it is merely a combination of agreeable sounds, to please our sense of hearing, and to tickle our nerves more or less. "It does not refine," he says; "it does not elevate; it does not strengthen. It leaves the moral nature quite untouched. It has no moral, —nay, no intellectual influence."

While we possess many technical and æsthetical works on architecture, sculpture, painting, and poetry, within the comprehension of the general public, music has, as yet, to struggle, in order to find its due and true place. That which, in a great measure, accounts for this state of things is the one-sided education of our musicians themselves; in general, at least. Their whole attention is directed, in most instances, towards the technical side of musical art. Their appreciation of the history, the philosophy, of their art, is a dark, indistinct understanding and presentiment; and many of the false theories about music are due, in a great extent, to their want of a more general knowledge and logical power. Thus, the æsthetical side of music is entirely in the hands of philosophers and speculative authors, who have, unfortunately, not the necessary technical musical education, and whose theories, therefore, are built on sand. Or else it rests in the hands of amateur authors, who write about the art as their fancies lead them. Of course there are, everywhere, honorable exceptions.

* * * * *

Music is not an isolated art. It forms a most necessary link in the great family of arts. Its origin is to be looked for at the same source as that of the other arts. Its ideal functions are also the same.

Art, in general, is that magic instrumentality by means of which man's mind reveals to man's senses that great mystery, the *beautiful*. The eye sees it; the ear hears it; the mind conceives it; our whole being feels the breath of God:

but to penetrate, in its full signification, that mystery, that charm which the beautiful thus exercises over us, is to penetrate the inconceivable ways of God. The sense of the beautiful is that God-like spark which the Creator has placed in the soul of man; and the necessity of giving it reality is that irresistible power which makes man an artist.

Not through one art-form alone does the idea of the beautiful reveal itself to us, but, as in the whole creation, through many-sidedness. Though different in their forms, which are necessarily dictated by the material which every species of art employs in order to express itself, yet the one idea of the beautiful is contained in all art.

To say that it requires more genius to create master-works in one art than in another is certainly a wrong assertion. Shakspeare, Beethoven, Michael Angelo, Phidias, — who can prove which one of these minds was the greatest?

In the plastic arts, the idea of the beautiful is expressed through outward forms. The eye serves the mind as interpreter of that ideal of which the artist finds models in the nature which surrounds him.

In music, the world, with its emotions and feelings, is driven back on the heart. The ideal of the artist thus rests in his own bosom. The idea of the beautiful is expressed through tone-forms, which the ear reveals to our mind. Thus, though deeply felt by every man, music's real nature is less understood than the more realistic plastic arts; hence the dualism of which I have spoken before.

In poetry, the objective nature of the plastic arts and the subjectivity of music are, in an ideal sense, united. In reading the description of a palace, of a beautiful figure, of a landscape, our mind sees those objects in great reality, while, at the same time, the peculiar mood in which these pictures, when associated with certain lyric and tragic situations, place us, thrills our soul with emotions and feelings in a great degree similar to those awakened by music.

Thus the aim of all arts is the same, though every one of them arrives at its own ends by different roads. Every one of them possesses, more or less, its moral, refining, ennobling qualities; every one of them can also be made the vehicle of demoralization, or to serve frivolous purposes. It is the true artist's mission to keep his ideal of the beautiful, in all its forms, chaste and pure. Not by descending to the level of every day's trivialities, will he fulfil this noble mission, but by lifting up his eyes towards the purifying atmosphere of the God-like ideal.

Art is a wonderful mirror of man's intellectual and sensual life, elevated into the regions of the beautiful. Its influence upon man's mind is thus ennobling, strengthening, elevating. Music is a member, and not the least, in the family of arts.

* * * * *

It has been my endeavor, in the following lectures, to throw light on those early periods of musical art, scarcely known or appreciated by amateurs, — and perhaps I do not exaggerate if I say, by the great majority of musicians also. And yet how important is it, for the understanding of our modern art-culture (if a sound and reliable judgment is to be gained), to possess a fair knowledge of the growth and development of musical forms. Besides the instruction this study affords, what a source of intellectual and artistic enjoyment it presents. We, at the same time, follow and observe the different changes of forms which the human mind creates, in order to express its feelings and emotions as influenced by the current thoughts of particular times. Music is a great, and, in many respects, a reliable guide in the study of human progress and development. No art is more closely connected with the inner life of man than music, whose magic power steps in at precisely the point where the positive expression of language fails.

The very essence of man's existence, it participates in its struggles, triumphs, reverses, and necessarily in its forms and expressions resembles those different phases.

Every one conversant with the literature of musical history will see that the plan and execution of the present work is an original one. It struck me, that, in this way, each distinct stage of development of the great epochs and art-forms would be more easily comprehended. Nor have I rested it solely on metaphysical speculations. I have tried its efficiency through practical experience. The outlines of this form ripened in preparing and planning, with Madame Raymond-Ritter, the "Historical Recitals" which were given by her and other artists, and which we destined to serve as æsthetical illustrations of different remarkable schools and periods of musical art. No little share of any satisfaction which my readers may derive from this work will be owing to my dear wife and sister artist, whose genuine enthusiasm, encouragement, taste, and practical assistance, have proved so valuable an inspiration to me while carrying out my plan, — a plan the more difficult, on account of my having undertaken to embody it in a, to me, foreign language.

* * * * *

I never was prejudiced or influenced, in speaking of the different masters, by the nationality, or the school, to which they or their labors belonged. I strove, as much as lay in my power, to deduce, from those of their works which were accessible to me, their individual importance as influencing and directing the growth of life and art. I never accepted any judgment, any opinion, of an important historical fact, or æsthetic appreciation of important works, that marked or prepared an era in music, until after a conscientious, careful examination, comparison, and study of the most reliable sources which were at my disposal, and most of which are in my own possession. (This I need hardly say, for the almost utter want of musical libraries and of private collections, on this continent, is a well-known fact, and a frequent subject of remark and regret among students.)

Though, according to my adopted plan, I was, in a certain sense, limited as to time and space, I endeavored to present a comprehensive and complete picture of each important epoch in our art. It was not my aim to entertain my reader, merely, with the enumeration of names and dates, but to bring him in lively and intellectual contact with, and relation to, the still, in many respects, mysterious means and ways which that beautiful art employs to reach its own ends and to fulfil its mission.

My book, therefore, does not pretend to be an exhaustive history of music, but, rather, a friendly, and, I trust, a thoroughly reliable, guide, to incite and direct those musical students who feel the desire, the want, of a deeper and more general knowledge of, and information as to, the growth and progress of their art than is common; to encourage and strengthen the talented, the striving one, in his unavoidably arduous and difficult labors and struggles; to point out to the timid and undecided the imperative and necessary duties of the true artist; to hold up a faithful mirror of art-life to the inexperienced, impatient aspirant for artistic fame.

* * * * *

But, alas! how many stop on the path that leads to the temple of art, to think of the great minds that prepared that path for them, and who not seldom, amidst the greatest trials and mental sufferings, poured out for us that cup of delight which men empty, time after time, in *naïve* and ungrateful ignorance? How many of those whose business it should be to see a little farther than the narrow walls of their own being, feel any desire to understand the historical development of their art? And yet, without this understanding, how is a broad musical culture to be gained? how is the sure foundation of future progress to be secured?

I shall often have occasion, in the course of my lectures, to point out the great industry, the iron perseverance, and the deep devotion displayed by our most eminent masters, not alone in creating original works after works, but also in studying, with the utmost diligence and thoroughness, the works of their predecessors. They knew how to respect the good qualities of those who lived and toiled before them, as well as those of their contemporaries. And they had not the same advantages that we have, in being able to procure for little money the model scores inevitably necessary to the student. They were forced to copy the good compositions that chance threw in their way. But in this manner they gained that great mastery in the technical execution of all the different arts of counterpoint which enabled them to write such quantities of perfect works. It was not all genius that made these masters so great, as many are led to believe: their eminence was also, and in no small measure, the result of persevering, continual, well-directed, deep study of the fundamental rules and principles of their art. Has not one of the most gifted poets and industrious men that ever lived — Goethe — said, that "genius is only another word for industry"? Only when a sure basis was gained by such industry, did they begin to improve upon the old forms, and become able to create new ones. They did not set up for critics while they were still scholars; they did not attempt to become innovators before they knew the alphabet of their art. Read the reliable biographies of eminent composers; study their own utterances about their art,—how they clung to their adopted good principles. Before giving way to pecuniary inducements, they first satisfied their sense of duty as artists. How is it in this respect with our young students? Scarcely yet able to write a succession of common chords with grammatical correctness, they already besiege the publisher. They have neither time nor perseverance to go through the necessary preliminary, earnest studies. They are all geniuses (much-abused title!); and geniuses do not need, they think, to study. They create and dictate their own laws; but they generally awaken too late from their delusive dream. A few years ago, a young man of this city came to ask my advice as to becoming a musician and a composer. He had some trifles, and a mass in manuscript, with him. I discovered in these crude productions some promising talent, and gladly laid out a plan of study for him, based on our European ideas of what is required from a composer. The young man was astonished at the severity and length of study required, and said to me. "Don't you think.

that, if I should work very hard for two years, I would be able to compose an opera like 'Trovatore,' or a 'Requiem' like Mozart's, and then make a great deal of money by it?"

I have since sought to hear tidings of the new Trovatore and the Requiem, but, so far, unsuccessfully. This is only one of many examples I could give. The genuine masters took delight in work itself, and waited patiently for their reward: our young aspirants would like to take the reward first, and to dispense with the drudgery altogether.

* * * * *

Thus far the present series of lectures embraces the following distinct epochs:—

FIRST LECTURE.

The Gregorian Chant, the Folk-song, Troubadour-song, and the invention of harmony; from the Christian era to the latter part of the fourteenth century.

SECOND LECTURE.

The old Flemish, German, English, Italian and Spanish schools (the great epoch of Catholic church-music and the Madrigal); from the latter part of the fourteenth century to the death of Palestrina.

THIRD LECTURE.

The Oratorio, including the Passion, the Mystery, and Miracle plays, and Protestant church-music; from the twelfth century to the death of Schumann.

FOURTH LECTURE.

The Opera, from its first invention in Italy to the death of Gluck.

FIFTH LECTURE.

The development of instrumental music; from the sixteenth century to Haydn.

I hope to be able to offer, in the course of next season, a second and closing series, which will include, Catholic and English-Protestant church-music, from the death of Palestrina to our own time; The modern opera after Gluck; Instrumental music since Ph. E. Bach and Haydn to our own day; also a historical sketch of music in America; and a succinct history of the literature of musical art. This will cover the whole field of musical history, treated as fully as possible in the form and limits I have selected. An alphabetic index of the principal subjects treated of in the work will also be added to the second series.

FREDERIC LOUIS RITTER.

NEW YORK, Sept. 1, 1870.

HISTORY OF MUSIC.

FIRST LECTURE.

The Gregorian Chant. — The Folk-song. — The Invention of Harmony, and the Troubadours. — From the Christian Era to the latter part of the Fourteenth Century.

THE cradle of music as an art, in the sense *we* understand it to-day, may be traced back to that of Christianity. The Old World had fulfilled its destiny, and the good tidings of the new gospel were heard in Palestine: the hopes of a future and a better life filled the hearts of men.

With Christianity, a new civilization gradually took the place of that of the Romans: the internal corruption of the Roman empire hastened its downfall, and undermined all that which even the continual invasions of barbarians had spared. With the new religion, men's thoughts were led to nobler, loftier aspirations the idea of a loving, pardoning God inspired them.

Music, the deeper expression of men's emotions and joys, found then a more fructifying field to take root in; and, with the growth of Christianity, music, as an eminently Christian art, began to flourish, and accompanied, as a faithful servant, the altars of the new gospel.

We have no real knowledge of the exact character of the music which formed a part of the religious devotion of the first Christian congregations. It was, however, purely vocal. Instrumental music was excluded, at first, from the church service. It was despised, as having been used by the Romans at their depraved festivities; and every thing reminding them of heathen worship could not be endured by the new religionists. As late as the fourth century, St. Hieronimus says, speaking of the degraded state of Roman spectacles, "A Christian maid should not know what a lyre or a flute is, and what their use is." This strict confinement to purely vocal music was, however, more adhered to in the churches of the Occident; for in the Orient, with the multiplication of Christian congregations, the custom of introducing instrumental music in the church service, after the manner of the heathen, became more and more general.

It is presumed that some of the hymns and psalms of the early Christians were taken from the Hebrew temple service, and some were of Greek origin. The peculiar versification of the Psalms gave rise to the *antiphonal* or *alternate chant*, sung by priests and people. This form, being also used at the services of the Greek temple, was no doubt imitated by the Oriental Christians; and from them it found its way to the churches of the Occident. How much the first Christians loved their hymns and singing, and resolved not to abandon them, even amid the greatest persecutions they were at first exposed to, is proven by a passage of Plinius from the beginning of the second century. He says, "On certain days, they will assemble before sunrise, and sing alternately (antiphonal) the praise of their God." And another writer, speaking of the sect of Therapeutists, says, "After supper, their sacred songs began. When all were arisen, they selected from the rest two choirs, — one of men, and one of women, — in order to celebrate some festival; and from each of these a person of a majestic form, and well skilled in music, was chosen to lead the band. They then chanted hymns in honor of God, composed in different measures and modulations, now singing together, and now answering each other by turns."

Also that persons of all ages and of both sexes participated in the singing of psalms and hymns, is proven by a passage of St. Eusebius; where, speaking of the consecration of the new churches, he says, "that there was one common consent in chanting forth the praises of God: the performance of the service was exact; the rites of the church were decent and majestic; and there was a place appointed for those who sang psalms, — *youths* and *virgins*, *old men* and *young*."

The more the new religion found disciples, the more it was found necessary to bring unity into the form of the church service: and, as singing of hymns and psalms formed a principal part in it, St. Ambrose, Bishop of Milan from 374 to 397, not only encouraged the setting and composing of hymns, but he also collected many among those already in use; and history attributes to him the having chosen and fixed four diatonic scales, as foundation for the music of the hymns. The following are said to be those scales: —

1. Authentic Keys, or Scales.

which are called, after him, *Ambrosian ecclesiastical keys.* St. Ambrose was a warm admirer of music, and is said to have written the words of many hymns. The celebrated "Te Deum Laudamus," however, is erroneously attributed to him: it is of Oriental origin, and probably adapted from the Greek Church. St. Augustine, the friend of St. Ambrose, speaks of the great delight he received in hearing the singing of hymns and psalms at the church of Milan, in the following terms: "The voices flowed in at my ears, truth was distilled into my heart, and the affection of piety overflowed in sweet tears of joy!"

But in those times, though new Christian churches sprang up everywhere amidst persecution, it was not yet possible to preserve a uniform manner in the music, which made such an essential part of the service. The melodies and chants of St. Ambrose changed, and lost much of their primitive purity.

It was then reserved to St. Gregory the Great who was at the head of the Christian Church from 591 to 604, to reform and regenerate the entire musical part of the church service.

St. Gregory was not only full of religious enthusiasm, but he was also fond of, and a connoisseur in, music. He collected the best hymns existing, is said to have written and composed many himself, arranged the liturgy for the Christian service according to the Church year, and had the whole written in a book, called an Antiphonar, which he deposited upon the altar of St. Peter, fastened with a chain, and which he intended to serve as a foundation and unchangeable direction for all time to come. This Gregorian chant is also called *cantus firmus*, or *cantus planus*. St. Gregory added to the four scales ascribed to St. Ambrose four more, calling the first *authentic*, and the others *plagal*. Here are the four plagal scales: —

2. Plagal Keys, or Scales.

These ecclesiastical keys, or scales, as established or accepted by St. Gregory, were thus distinguished: —

First tone D. Dorian.
Second tone A. Æolian.
Third tone E. Phrygian.
Fourth tone B. Hypophrygian.
Fifth tone F. Lydian.
Sixth tone C. Ionian.
Seventh tone G. Mixolydian.
Eighth tone D. Dorian.

It was not until the sixteenth century that the Greek names were affixed to these keys, principally through the teachings of Glareanus.

It is presumed, and, indeed, admitted, by many modern writers on music, that the scales which St. Ambrose and St. Gregory laid as the foundation for the melodies and chants of their hymns and psalms were taken from the musical system of the Greeks.

St. Gregory, whose influence was so beneficial to the advancement of true church music, worked unceasingly for its introduction and study. He erected singing-schools in Rome, and was himself often present, and watched the instruction. The characters which St. Gregory used to note the chants of the Antiphonar were the *neumæ*,— small crooks and strokes of various shapes and positions, placed over the words to designate the pitch and the duration of the sound. When these signs were used without lines, they must have been very uncertain guides; and an old author says, "These irregular signs must have been productive of more error than science, as they were often so carelessly and promiscuously placed, that, while one was singing a semitone or a fourth, others would sing a third or a fifth." In the course of the next century, one line was first used; and then two lines were drawn, and the places of the *neumæ* were thus fixed with more certainty. The Gregorian chant soon found its way to other countries where the Christian religion took the place of heathen worship: in 604 and 606, Roman singers appeared in Gaul and Britanny; and, in the latter country, vocal music especially flourished. In 752, Pope Stephen II. sent twelve singers to Pepin of France; and in Germany, where the conversion of the heathen was vigorously pushed forward, the apostle St. Boniface founded several singing-schools at the seats of bishops and in convents. But very often these schools only succeeded as long as those enthusiastic apostles were at the head of them: if they died, the people would fall back again into their wild and barbarous state. John Diaconus, the biographer of St. Gregory, says, that, among all European nations, the Gauls and the Alemanni were the least fitted to understand and execute the Gregorian chant in its purity; because they would always mix it up with some of their own. "Their rough voices, roaring like thunder, are not capable of soft modulation; for their throats, hardened by drink, cannot execute with flexibility what a tender melody requires. Indeed, their voices give out tones similar to the rumbling of a baggage-wagon rolling down from a height; and, instead of touching the hearts of their hearers, they only fill them with aversion."

Under the reign of Charlemagne, from 768 to 814, church music made great progress in the different countries of his great empire. Charlemagne, who was so powerful a support of the Christian religion, was very fond of music; and the singing of hymns and psalms was zealously taught at his high-schools, and very often under his own supervision. To preserve the Gregorian liturgical manner of singing in its purity, and to realize unity in the service of the different churches of his empire, he had singing-masters sent from Rome at different times, and erected singing-schools at Metz and Soissons. Charlemagne himself paid several visits to the pope in Rome. There always existed disputes and jealousies between the Roman and Gallic singers, as to whom should belong the right to sing at the emperor's service while in Rome.

"The French pretended to sing better and more agreeably than the Italians; and the Italians, on the contrary, regarding themselves as more learned in ecclesiastical music, which they had been taught by St. Gregory (or, rather, according to the true tradition of St. Gregory's teachings), accused their competitors of corrupting, disfiguring, and spoiling the true chant. The dispute being brought before the emperor, the French, thinking themselves sure of his countenance, insulted the Roman singers, who, on their part, emboldened by superior knowledge, and comparing the musical abilities of their great master, St. Gregory, with the ignorance and rusticity of their rivals, treated them as fools and barbarians. As their altercation was not likely to come to a speedy issue, the most pious emperor, Charles, asked his chanters which they thought to be the purest and best water, that which was drawn from the source at the fountain-head, or that, which, after being mixed with turbid and muddy rivulets, was found at a great distance from the original spring? They cried out, unanimously, that all water must be most pure at the source: upon which the Emperor said, 'Mount ye, then, up to the pure fountain of St. Gregory, whose chant ye have manifestly corrupted.' "

All that we know of the state of music, till up to the ninth century, shows that all the hymns and psalms were single-voiced, — that is to say, sung in unison; although some few rare efforts towards discovering and introducing harmony — that is, the singing of various parts simultaneously — were made by different learned and industrious monks in their solitude.

It would lead me too far to relate here all the learned historical speculations of this or that savant, whether it was the Celtic or German race that first made use of harmony. The hypothesis that it was most probably invented by the Celts is based on the following fact: this people possessed, among other musical instruments, a kind of violin, in a primitive and rough state, called Rotta, Grwth, Crotta, &c. The instrument was overstrung with several strings of different pitch, and it was played with a bow. This leads very naturally to the supposition that it was more than probable that chords could be drawn from the Grwth. With the little light history and science have as yet thrown on this subject, it is difficult to trace from the use of the Grwth the gradual introduction of harmony in music, as a form which stamps our musical art, at the same time, as entirely different from that of the old world. It seems, however, safe to admit the fact, that with the migration of the northern tribes into the southern provinces of Europe, and their final settlement there, harmonious music became gradually known and practised.

The oldest historical document of which we have any knowledge, on harmony, in the modern acceptation of the term, is by *Isidore*, Archbishop of Seville, who lived at the time of St. Gregory (from 570 to 636), and whose friend he was. Isidore says, in his "Sentences on Music," "Harmonious music is a modulation of the voice: it is also the union of simultaneous sounds." He also speaks of two kinds of harmony, *Symphony* and *Diaphony*. By the first word he meant probably a combination of consonant, and by the latter of dissonant intervals. Though we possess here explicit rules for the use of harmony, it took several centuries of labor and experiment before men were able to create works, even in a simple sense, in which melody and harmony concurred to give adequate enjoyment. The state of society, and the continual invasions of barbarians into the Roman empire, devastating all that opposed their passage, hindered the peaceful cultivation of arts and sciences, — all intellectual life remaining, so to speak, in suspense; and communications were then so scarce, that even the improvements which some monks made, scarcely went farther than the walls of their own monastery. Thus the soil was not advantageous to the progress of music, although the musical liturgy was enriched, during this period, by many new chants. But, without gradual perfection and use of harmony, musical art, in our sense, would have remained stationary, partaking the fate of Greek music, and less rich in rhythm. Greek music, as far as we understand it, closely followed the rhythm of that rich language: "being especially vocal, it was every where governed by the peculiarity of the syllables, and, therefore, reduced to fixed limits. We are, throughout, led to the opinion, that there existed a great harmony between the poetical and musical composition of the Greeks; that is to say, they never wedded to the text a music, which, being perhaps beautiful in itself, forced and distorted the words and syllables, and thus rendered the meaning of this text obscure, and a mere play of sound." * In the Gregorian chant, notes of equal value accompanied the different syllables; but it cannot be said that it was void of all rhythm, as, in execution, the proper accents of the words were always considered. St. Gregory certainly chose this manner of chanting, as being more majestic, more solemn, more adapted to the worship of a large Christian congregation. Although apparently monotonous, the Gregorian chant bore within itself the germ of a more melodious independence than the so much praised Greek music, as it did not follow the syllables in such a slavish manner; for we already find groups of many notes sung as ornaments upon certain vowels, principally at the close of sentences in masses, hymns, and psalms. The great influence and importance of the Gregorian chant in music, regarded as the modern Christian art, cannot be too highly estimated. A freer tone-life began to reveal itself in the art of song under St. Gregory: from the life of sentiment, deepened

* Dr. John H. Schmidt: Die antike Compositions lehre.

and enriched by the inspiring influence of Christianity, sprang a more independent tone-speech. A tone-language, indeed, "in which *faith*, *belief*, and *feeling* expressed themselves in such a manner, that, in St. Gregory's time, it was said that the holy man had received from a higher spiritual world the power of creating such songs." The Gregorian chant is the central point from which all older compositions for the Catholic Church proceeded, and upon which they rested. The classic forms of the old masses, motets, and hymns, including the works of Palestrina and his school, sprang from the Gregorian chant. In fact, it will remain the foundation of all true Catholic church-music.

It needed only one step, and the solid foundation of that beautiful art-temple, which stands in its wonderful glory before us to-day, would be laid; and this step was the discovery of harmony, and its general use in the practice of choral music.

The first author known to us as having left a treatise on harmony, in which the rules are illustrated, at the same time, by practical examples, was a Flemish monk, *Hucbald* of St. Amand, in Flanders, who lived at the end of the ninth and at the beginning of the tenth centuries. In Hucbald's time, music in several parts, called to-day "polyphonic," was not yet known by the term "harmonious music," or "harmony," but by that of "organum," or "diaphony." The intervals which composed these parts were called "symphonies." The specimens which the learned monk gives us of the harmony or organum in use in his time are very crude, and sound to our ears not very pleasant; as he employed, and, according to the renowned old Greek system, allowed, only a succession of perfect consonants, which are the *fourth*, the *fifth*, and the *octave*. One would not trust his ears on hearing the organum of Hucbald, but would think it impossible that such had ever been in practice; yet it seems there is no doubt about it. The good monk himself, in giving the necessary rules for employing the *symphonies*, or intervals, in composing the organum, recommends them as sweet and agreeable in their effect upon the ear.* Here is one of his specimens as an example:—

3.

* Though this form of Hucbald's organum has been admitted by al. the most reliable musical historians, Dr. O. Paul maintains that the organum is a sort of counterpoint, in which one voice imitates the other in the octave, the fifth, and fourth. If this explanation of the organum is to be admitted, then great injustice has been done to our venerable old author. The subject, however, has not yet been cleared up.

In the dark days of the middle ages, the monks, in whose hands the meagre cultivation of literature and science then almost exclusively rested, and who slavishly followed — as much as their knowledge would allow them — the works of Greek and Roman authors, tried, for centuries, to deduce their rules for the science of music from what they could gather at the same source; but the author considered for a long time as the oracle by musical writers was *Boethius* (from about 476 to 525.) There was a hard and long struggle, however, between the theory and practice of music. The Christian singers, led by empiricism, admitted and introduced forms in their songs which did not accord with the rules of Greek authors and Boethius; hence the confusion and complications which rested heavily upon the progress of musical art. It is, therefore, not astonishing when we read that it took half a man's life-time to make himself master of the rudiments of music in those days, as the rules were so many and difficult to learn. It was then thought that no one could be a good teacher of philosophy or theology, without possessing a knowledge of music. Under these circumstances, it was well that a man appeared, who, endowed with great practical sense, partly removed these difficulties, created a new and simpler method of teaching, and brought musical notation to greater perfection. This teacher was *Guido of Arezzo*, who lived in the early part of the eleventh century, and was a monk in the Benedictine monastery in Pomposa, in Italy. Guido, like St. Gregory and Hucbald, probably, also used the letters A, B, C, D, E, F, G, to designate the tones of the scale, and the *neumœ* as musical characters. A really great merit of his was that of adding two more lines to those already existing, and thus giving the *neumœ* a more fixed place. Two of the four lines were black: of the other two, the second of the four lines was red, the fourth was yellow, and sometimes green. The red line fixed the tone F, the yellow the tone C. From this dates the use of our F, or bass clef, and the C clef.

Guido was a good practical teacher, and was accustomed to explain by word of mouth many of the existing difficulties in musical practice. A proof of this is, that he enabled his pupils, in a comparatively short time, to read any chant at first sight, which the other singers never could do in all their lives. He is also the originator of the solmization by means of the syllables *ut*, *re*, *mi*, *fa*, *sol*, *la*. To teach singing at first sight to his pupils, Guido used an air which was so peculiarly constructed that every other line (verse) began with a tone one degree higher than the previous one: the first commenced on C, the next on D, the third on E, the fourth on F, the fifth on G, the sixth on A. The writing of the Sapphic strophe is attributed to Paul Diaconus, who was a contemporary of Charlemagne (730–800). Here is the hymn:

4.

Every profession in those days had its patron, and, St. John being then worshipped as the patron of singers, this hymn was sung in his honor, and was considered a remedy against hoarseness. The so-called *Guidonian hand*, by means of which solmization and the ecclesiastical keys were taught, in those times, calling the top of the thumb Gamma (G), and applying the names of the rest of the notes to the joints of each finger, is also ascribed to him, though perhaps erroneously, as it more probably owes its origin and development to some of his disciples. It found its way to all countries of Europe, and contributed much towards the study of musical theory. As a harmonist, Guido did not go much beyond Hucbald. No teacher or musical author obtained such a popular reputation after his death as Guido: all that was taught, improved, invented, in musical branches, through the eleventh, twelfth, thirteenth, and fourteenth centuries, was attributed to him. "Guido," says Burney, "is one of those favored names, to which the liberality of posterity sets no bounds. He has long been regarded, in the empire of music, as *lord of the manor*, to whom all strays revert, — not indeed as chattels to which he is known to have an inherent right and natural title, but such as accident has put into the power of his benefactors; and when once mankind has acquired a habit of generosity, unlimited by envy and rival claims, they wait not till the plate or charity box is held out to them, but give freely and unsolicited whatever they find without loss or effort."

With the experience and facility church-singers gained, no doubt Hucbald's and Guido's organum, or diaphony, would not always satisfy them; and a species of harmony sprang up, — although it existed at first only in practice, — which exercised a great influence upon music of simultaneous sound, and even upon the organum itself. This was the *discantus* or *counterpoint* (as it was afterwards called), at the end of the eleventh, or at the commencement of the twelfth, centuries. The *cantus firmus* or *cantus planus* of St. Gregory, and in its crude harmonizations in the organum, consisted of notes of equal value. In executing these chants, they were either sung in unison, or, as in the organum, the parts moved closely together. The *neumæ*, the musical characters of this epoch, were found sufficient to determine the pitch of the tones for the singers, as rhythm and measure, in our sense, were not yet observed. In the *discantus* (descant), which consisted of two or more parts, a given melody, generally a Gregorian chant, called *tenor* (that is, "to hold"), formed the foundation; and, accompanying it, one, two or three parts were invented, probably first improvised. The different parts which composed the descant were not always sung in tones of the same value, like the organum. To keep these parts together in a tolerably harmonious manner, it was, no doubt, soon discovered that a certain understanding was necessary respecting the value of the different notes representing the tones, and the time they were to be sung in. All this led to the discovery of measured music, or the *time-table*,—*mensural music*, as it was then called. Through frequent practising and experimentalizing, the ears of singers became more and more sensibie to the disagreeable and barbarous effect of a continual succession of fourths, fifths, and octaves, as we find in the organum. Thirds and sixths being excluded from practical use by the old Greek system, the theorists of all this epoch, slavish imitators of the renowned Greek system, excluded them also. But in closely pursuing the progress of musical art, as much as the meagre documents left to us of those dark times allow, we must admit, that, in practice, singers were far ahead of the theorists; and, step by step, these latter had to record, and — which is their real merit — systemize for further use and development, that which others found, or admitted through tradition. In this way, the real meaning of consonances and dissonances, and a more appropriate and effective use of them, must, indeed, have been known long before writers on music acquainted us with the change. *Franco de Cologne* is considered the earliest writer on mensural music. He lived in the beginning of the thirteenth century. In his work on music, "*Musica et Ars Cantus Mensurabilis*," he speaks of the different value of the notes.

Formerly there were only two, — *longa*, ■, and *brevis*, ■: he already has four, with the corresponding rests, — *duplex longa*, ■, *longa*, *brevis*, and *semi-brevis*, ◆.

5. Rests.

Perfect Longa, three beats. Imperfect Longa, two beats.

Brevis. Semi-brevis. Final pause.

He also mentions two kinds of time,—the *perfect* and the *imperfect*. Triple time he calls perfect (trinity being the substance of all perfection), and common time was imperfect. The bars, as indicating the measures, were not yet in use: a longa and a brevis representing three, and a longa two, the singers counted according to the value of these notes. In the explanations he gives of the consonances and dissonances, and in the use of them, Franco already approximates to our ideas of them, although he still ranks the sixths among dissonances. The description and rules he gives of the discantus, in three, four, and five parts, show an immense progress over the old organum.

Mensural music, as explained and probably perfected by Franco, was gradually introduced and adopted by church-singers and theorists. A marked distinction began already to be established, in the treatises on music, between mensural music as a species, and the *cantus planus* of St. Gregory. It found its way, and was cultivated with great success, in England, very soon after Franco's teachings. Commentators on Franco's works — or, at least, theorists who took Franco's works as a basis, although they do not show great progress beyond him — were *Walter Odington* of Evesham, under the reign of Henry III., and *Hieronimus de Moravia*, about 1260. Of more importance to the development of mensural music and harmony were *Marchetto di Padua*, in the latter part of the twelfth, and at the beginning of the thirteenth centuries; and *Jean de Muris*, about 1330, doctor of the Sorbonne at Paris, famous as a philosopher, mathematician, and writer on music. Many of the rules he gave for the use of consonant and dissonant intervals in polyphonic writing still possess value.

As I shall often have occasion to make use of the expressions "consonance" and "dissonance," I will here give the explanation of those terms. The difference between two musical sounds, or tones, as regards their pitch, is called an "interval." The nature of the sound produced by two or more intervals, when sung or played together, is either consonant or dissonant. Franco explained consonance and dissonance in the following manner, which explanation, indeed, sufficed for theorists until our day: "Two or more voices or parts, harmonizing, when sung together.

in a manner agreeable to the ear, form a consonance. Dissonance, on the contrary, when two parts are united so as to sound disagreeable to the ear." Now, consonant means, in general, agreeable; dissonant, disagreeable: but as, in a more particular sense, the materials out of which our musical harmony is formed can never be disagreeable without ceasing to be music, we must find a more generic explanation of consonant and dissonant intervals. Every tone is the product of a certain number of vibrations, either through the human voice, or through artificial means. If, in sounding two different tones simultaneously, the number of vibrations of the one is in a simple proportion to the number of vibrations of the other, then the ear receives the sound in a satisfactory manner, and we term such intervals "consonances" (for the ear, like the mind, sooner comprehends that which is of simple proportion): the octave is like 1 to 2; the fifth, 2 : 3; the fourth, 3 : 4; the major third, 4 : 5; the major sixth, 3 : 5; the minor third, 5 : 6; the minor sixth, 5 : 8. These intervals are all more or less perfect consonances. If, on the other hand, the number of vibrations of two different tones is so multiplied as to render their relative proportions more complicated, then the ear receives the sound in an unsatisfactory manner, and we term the intervals thus produced, "dissonance;" the major second, 8 : 9. and 9 : 10; the minor second, 15 : 16; the major seventh, 8 : 15; the minor seventh, 9 : 16, &c. (The two figures represent two tones: during the same period of time the first tone vibrates, say three times, the second vibrates four times, &c.) Now, all the different intervals which musical practice has admitted, form a gradual chain of more or less satisfactory sounds, from the restful and most perfect consonance, to the sharpest, most restless, and exciting dissonance. Their skilful use, based upon a true musical sentiment, and thorough study of the nature of these different intervals, plays a most important part in the true composer's productions. "The dissonances," ingeniously says Printz, in his "Phrynis" (1696), "are the darkness, the consonances the light: the light would not be as agreeable to us if it were always day and never night. The dissonances are the bitter, the consonances the sweet: the sweet would never be as agreeable if we had not also tasted the bitter."

There also existed in the middle ages, besides the descant, another kind of counterpoint, or music in different parts, generally for three voices, which was called *falso-bordone*, or *faux-bourdon.*

This kind of harmony consisted of a succession of chords of the sixth, over a Gregorian chant, as *cantus firmus*.

6.

The falso-bordone seems to have originated in France, and was thence introduced in the pope's chapel. With the new discoveries and the greater facilities for mastering the material, no doubt many extravagances found their way into the manner of singing the *discantus*, or descant, to the displeasure of many a Christian: on the other hand, many, out of habit, clung to the old organum, and condemned the new descant as profanation of the divine service. So Pope John XXII., in the year 1322, issued a decree, at Avignon, in which he reminded the clergy of the proper manner in which church singing should be fixed; and, speaking of the disciples of the new school of music, says, "that those who were captivated with it, attending the *new* notes and *new* measures of the disciples of the new school, would rather have their ears tickled with semibreves and minims, and such frivolous inventions, than hear the ancient ecclesiastical chant." But, notwithstanding the frivolous invention, the descant and the falso-bordone found their way even to the pope's chapel, where they were cultivated with great success, and prepared the way for those great masterpieces of Josquin des Près, Orlandus Lassus, Palestrina, and many others, which afterwards adorned the Catholic Church.

We have seen, through the preceding narrative, that several centuries of labor, experiment, and in many cases, no doubt, of disappointment, passed until fixed rules for the general use of harmony were established. Nevertheless, those preliminary, long, and tedious labors were necessary, before men, gifted by the hand of God with genius, could create the glorious works that delight us; in which the whole power of melodious charm, wedded to rich and exquisite harmony, speaks to us in so sublime a language; a language never dreamed of by those monks, faithful and restless gatherers of the first crude and coy material, and who certainly thought wonders of the barbarous sounds of their beloved organum. But, thanks to the devotion and industry of these monks in their solitary cells, they saved the remains of the great intellectual life of old Greece and Rome from utter destruction, and, through their speculations and experiments in arts and sciences, often, no doubt, very pedantic and seemingly insignificant, unknowingly sowed the seed of many an art-form of which we reap the rich and delicious fruit to-day.

The *folk-song* is an outgrowth from the life of the people. It is a direct naturalistic efflux of popular lyric song; unassisted by art, it is true, but yet the product of innate artistic instinct in the people, seeking a more lofty expression than that of every-day speech for those feelings which are awakened in the soul by the varied events of life. The first authors of the folk-song are, with very few exceptions, unknown: they were either men and women of the people, who, with unembarrassed simplicity, and unaware of the laws of art, described, with free originality, that which lived and moved in the soul of the people; or they were artists, who were so inwardly connected with the people in their feelings and mode of expression, that their productions seem to spring from the same source. On one side purely human feeling, on the other side national character, are truthfully reflected in the folk-song: in it the characteristics of a nation are so faithfully displayed, that it not only betrays its origin, but also enables us to judge, through its distinguishing features, of the relationship existing between different races of men. The unwearying attraction of the folk-song consists of the freshness, originality, and unconcealed truthfulness with which every natural movement of the soul is expressed; nor is it only healthy realism that charms us in it. There we also find presentiments of a lofty, noble ideal, and such an exquisite sense of real poetic beauty, breaking through the rind of natural growth, as assures to the best of these songs an imperishable existence.

There is no doubt that the ancient nations — the Hebrews, the Greeks, the Romans, &c. — possessed many folk-songs: yet none of them, as far as we can judge, have come down to us; and, although it is presumed that some of these songs found their way into the Christian Church, history fails to give any distinct proof of it. Through the confusion caused in the political and social state of European nations by the migration of the German races in the fifth and sixth centuries, and through the uncertain state of the different languages mixed up with each other, the cultivation of poetry was out of the question; and, of course, secular music had as yet no foundation. It was not until a new civilization took the place of disorder and anarchy, that poetry and song began to adorn the homes of the new inhabitants.

In the history of the development of our European or Occidental music, — which in its forma tion is ruled by entirely different laws from those of the Oriental nations,—the folk-song is of the greatest importance. The folk-song and the Gregorian song are the two factors that form the foundation upon which all forms of our musical art rest. Though each one of them followed, in the course of time, altogether different roads, yet we shall see that they sometimes lend each other their individual charms. The Gregorian chant, creating its own peculiar tonalities,—the ecclesiastical keys,—and enriched by the invention of harmony, which gave to these tonalities a still more solemn, characteristic, church-like coloring, is thus at once distinct from any previous effort of temple music; at all events, as far as we can judge from the historical records transmitted to us on this subject. The Gregorian chant was thus raised to the highest form of art-song. The folk-song puts its whole signification in melodious expression, being limited to the more narrow circle of the *naïve* sentiment of the poetry which gives it meaning: human reality and emotion are its functions. The Gregorian chant points to the infinite beyond. The tonality of the folk-song, resting in general upon the key and the dominant, is simpler in its formal construction than that of the Gregorian chant.

Though old chronicles have preserved and transmitted to us the words of many a German,

Italian, French, and Spanish folk-song, popular at certain periods of the middle ages, yet the melodies of these songs have, unfortunately, not all been noted down, and are, therefore, not all known to us. What we possess of such melodies are, for the most part, from the latter half of the fourteenth century, when composers — contrapuntists, as they were called — made some of the most popular melodies the theme of their masses and motets. I shall speak, in my second lecture, of this peculiar manner. Many of the folk-songs of the Celtic races, such as the Scots, Irish, Welsh, and the Bretons of France, are undoubtedly of very ancient origin. A number of them must have existed long before the introduction of the Christian religion. In examining these original characteristic melodies, so full of a peculiar poetical charm, one cannot help wondering at the fact that these people never made a mark in the higher culture of music, and, as far as history records, never sent forth a composer in whose genius the art-world has found concentrated all the poetic individual characteristics of the musically-gifted Celtic race.

Belonging to another class of folk-song, but pointing already to the art-song, are the songs of the troubadours, the minstrels, and the minnesingers. It seems that the love for lyric poetry and song combined was first manifested by the counts and knights of the south of France, and especially by the nobles of Provence; for, in the twelfth century, the influence of the culture of poetry and song was already felt, as more refined manners began to regulate the barbarous customs of the warlike and quarrelsome barons. At the time of the Crusades, the order of the troubadours and minstrels augmented considerably all over Europe.

"In Provence, on the flowery shores of the Durance, in the land where Grecian culture, tended by the Romans, had never wholly been destroyed; where the arts of peace had long flourished, and yet more richly after the migrations of the nations, and in emulation of the Spanish Arabs; under the brilliant heaven of Southern France, where nature, womanly beauty, manly courage, and courtly manners lent their highest charms to life,—the luxuriant flower of lyric song sprang forth among the troubadours. It is true that the music and poetry of the troubadours was a natural outgrowth of that epoch of stirring life,—of love, longing, hatred, joy, and melancholy; but every mental growth demands its appropriate soil, and only in the highest circles could an appropriate field for lyric song then exist. Though the profession of singer had been regarded as an honorable one since the time of the Gallic bards, and though the jongleurs (musical and poetical conjurors, who travelled from castle to castle for the entertainment of barbarous chieftains) had preceded the troubadours, it was only towards the end of the eleventh century that it came to be considered as a matter of perhaps more consequence that a youthful knight should know how to compose, sing, and play, than that he should invent verses, and read and write correctly. The art of the troubadour was entitled the *gai saber* (or *gaie science*), and to the idea of gayety a noble meaning was attached. The true chevalier, it was said, should never lose his normal feeling of enthusiasm and joy: like an interior sun, the joy of love should illuminate his life, and continually excite him to noble actions and fortitude in trial, purifying his soul from envious, sombre sadness, from avarice, torpidity, and hardness of mind. Melancholy was regarded as a morbid feeling, born of scepticism and degeneracy, a want of power to accomplish great deeds or duties. Gayety, or joy, was a state of mind regarded by the troubadours as corresponding with that of religious grace. The end of their profession was the service of religion, honor, and woman, in deed and in song. One of their mottoes was, 'Love and religion protect all the virtues;' another ran, 'My soul to God, my life for the king, my heart for my lady, my honor for myself.'

"The troubadour most esteemed was he who could invent, compose, and accompany his own songs; but those who were unable to play the instruments of the period,—the harp, lute, viola, or citara (the ancient Irish rota or crowth),—were accompanied by a salaried minstrel: in the South, these minstrels were termed jongleurs, or violars. If a troubadour was not gifted with a fine voice, he employed a singer (cantador, or musar) to perform the songs which he could create, but not sing.

"The merit of the troubadours in furthering the progress of music as an art was, that they liberated melody from the fetters of calculation, gave it the stamp of individuality, and bore it on the wings of fancy into the domains of sentiment. They had the further merit of introducing new and peculiar rhythmic changes of time, which, apparently irregular, were really forcible, symmetrical, and original. It is also more than probable, that the troubadours received new ideas, in regard to melody, from the East; as they found, among the Arabs, not only a different system of tones, but many fanciful vocal ornaments, then unknown in Europe, and which they introduced in their own songs on their return from the Crusades. But, as harmony was in that day yet undeveloped, the flowing vine of melody received little support from it, and therefore often appears weak. The rules of composition were then highly complicated and ill-classified: yet they were well understood by the best-educated troubadours; and though their earlier songs were stiff, closely resembling the Gregorian chant in form and style, in some of the latter ones we find graceful melodies that leave little to be desired, and that possess more real variety and individuality of character than do the words attached to them. Their charm is, to the intelligent musician, unique, genuine, healthy, vigorous, and sweet as the songs of a choir of birds heard on a spring morning, in the heart of a fresh and dewy wood, when the wind is blowing and the sun shining." *

The most celebrated of the troubadours were *Adam de la Hale*, *Gaucem Faidit*, *Thibaut* (King of Navarre), and the *Chatelain de Coucy*. Quite a number of their songs have come down to us. Here is the music of two of Adam de la Hale's songs. The first is a descant, or counterpoint, set for three voices. Though crude and awkward in the harmonization, it already shows, in many respects, quite a progress in the difficult art of counterpoint. The sense of the words attached to this music is, "As long as I live I

* Fanny Raymond Ritter: Essay on the Troubadours, &c.

will love you, and never depart from my word.' The second, "Robin m'aime, Robin m'a demandé," is an air from an interesting little play called "Robin and Marion." This play may be considered as the earliest precursor of the opera. I need hardly say, that I have added the harmonization of this charming *chanson*. Adam de la Hale lived during the latter half of the thirteenth century.

7.

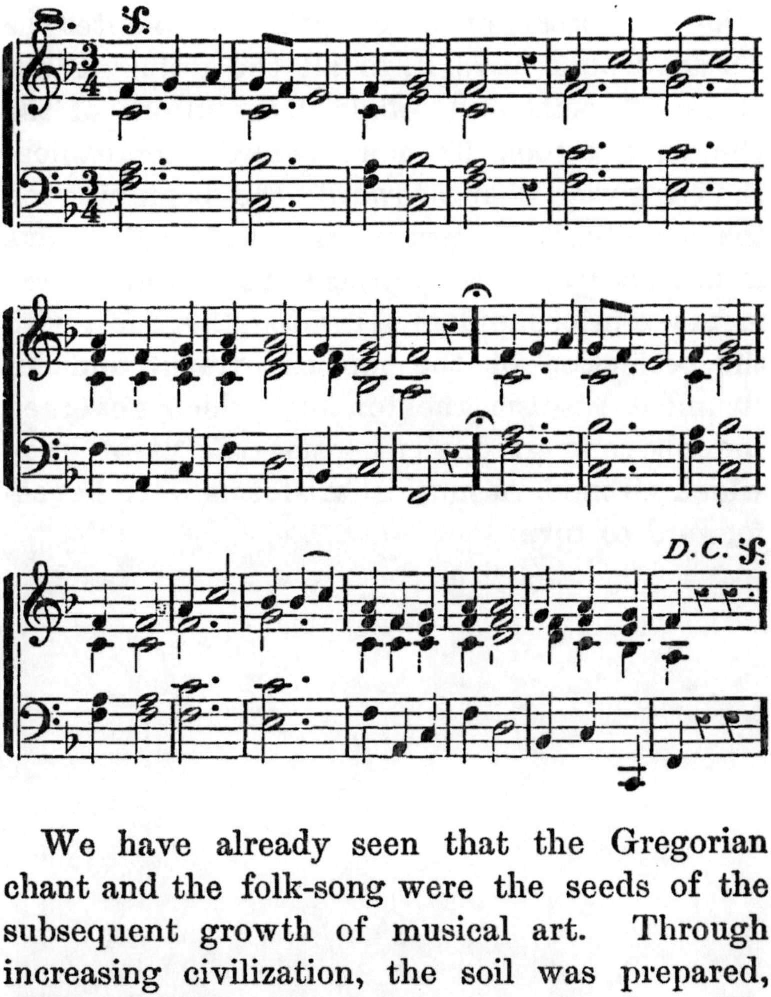

We have already seen that the Gregorian chant and the folk-song were the seeds of the subsequent growth of musical art. Through increasing civilization, the soil was prepared, little by little, to receive these seeds. The Church guarded and nourished, with solicitude, its own tender plant, — the Gregorian chant, — which, in the following century, shot forth strong branches, capable of producing wonderful fruit in the sixteenth century. The folk-song, long abandoned to itself, transplanted, as chance would have it, to all the different climates of social and religious evolutions of the people, overtook its more favored companion, the Gregorian chant, towards the beginning of the seventeenth century, and, as I shall prove in my lectures on the musical drama and instrumental music, supplanted it altogether; for, with the perfection of the musical drama and instrumental music, the tonality which governed the folk-song gradually became the pivot upon which all modern musical art-forms were henceforward to turn.

SECOND LECTURE.

The old Flemish, German, English, Italian, and Spanish schools (the great epoch of Catholic church-music, and the madrigal); from the fourteenth century to the death of Palestrina.

In my first lecture, I traced the timid, uncertain, and slow step of musical art, until it came somewhat near that which *we* call *music*. It was in its infancy; but the vigorous new life, the natural healthiness, the rich imagination which those Goths, those Franks, those Alemanni, those Saxons, — in two words, the *German element*, intensified and purified by the civilizing influence of Christianity, — infused into the more or less depraved nations of the demoralized Roman empire, was a fitting nourishment for music, the youngest member in the family of arts.

Until now, we have seen the different nations of Europe participating with equal success in the meagre cultivation of musical art, as it then existed. Towards the latter part of the four teenth century, however, the scene changes, and we perceive different nations taking the lead, sometimes for more than a century, and impressing their own individuality upon all styles of art-form. These nations were principally *the Netherlanders (Dutch)*, *the Italians*, and *the Germans.*

Though the power of the old Roman empire was annihilated, under the destructive strokes of the different German tribes, a new and no less powerful one began to subjugate the various new kingdoms; and that was *feudalism.* It may be, that the victorious tribes, then in process of formation and assimilation into nations, yet continually fighting among themselves, needed a hard lesson of humiliation and moral subordination, before their rough and awkward natures were fitted to appreciate and understand the advantages of the new civilization and religion: but it is certain that power was misused, and an endeavor was made to crush out liberty among the people. At the same time, we must give the Church the credit of having protected the tender germs of infant art and literature. Towards the latter part of the middle ages, the morning of a new and powerful intellectual life began to dawn. Renewed industry and commerce created wealth. In large and flourishing cities, the sense of liberty and independence from the pressure of feudalic rule united the citizens in powerful corporations. With wealth and liberty, literature, art, and science found a convenient and fructifying field. From Italy, the new light spread over the other European countries. The Italians, everywhere surrounded by the sublime remains of old Greek and Roman art, first awoke from the lethargy and confusion caused by that great migration of northern nations. In Bologna, Pisa, Padua, Parma, Naples. and other cities, universities and high-schools were founded, where, it is said, thousands of students from all countries flocked, to listen to the teaching of great masters; and, of this rich, healthy, and varied spectacle, *Dante* was the great and lofty central figure.

It is, however, curious to observe that Italy, the *alma mater* of all Europe in those times, received her first musical works of any importance from foreign composers. Foreign musicians, *Ultramontanes*, as they were called, stood at the head of her schools of music, chapels, and church choirs for more than a century; and these were principally Netherlanders. It seems that the inhabitants of the Low Countries first availed themselves of the advantages and blessings of more liberal institutions than the rest of Europe; and, industrious and enterprising as they were, the arts, principally music and painting, were early and passionately cultivated among them. Motley, in his "History of the Dutch Republic, gives the following picture: "Thus fifteen ages have passed away; and in the place of a horde of savages, living amongst swamps and thickets, swarm three millions of people, the most industrious, the most prosperous, perhaps the most intelligent, under the sun. Their cattle, grazing on the bottom of the sea, are the finest in Europe; their agricultural products of more exchangeable value than if Nature had made their land to overflow with wine and oil. Their navigators are the boldest, their mercantile marine the most powerful, their merchants the most enterprising in the world. Holland and Flanders, peopled by one race, vie with each other in the pursuits of civilization. The Flemish skill in mechanical and fine arts is unrivalled. Belgian musicians delight and instruct other nations. Belgian pencils have, for a century, caused the canvas to glow with colors and combinations never before seen."

Although French, Italian, German, and English composers at first contributed equally to the perfection of that art called counterpoint, thus far the merit of first producing works of a higher standard has been attributed to the Netherlanders. The school of music of the Netherlanders is generally divided into four different epochs, each one distinguished by that composer, who through his works, and his influence as a teacher, was foremost among his contemporaries. Thus, we have the epoch of *Dufay*, that of *Okeghem*, that of *Josquin des Près*, and that of *Willaert*.

The oldest masses, written in contrapuntal style, are to be found in the archives of the pope's chapel in Rome. Their author is *William Dufay*, who is said to have been born at Chimay in Hainault. Baini, in his biography of Palestrina, says that Dufay was a tenor singer in the Sixtine Chapel in Rome, from 1380 to 1432, and that he also died there. Another modern writer, T. W. Arnold, has, however, undertaken to prove* that the composer Dufay began to be celebrated not sooner than 1436, and that he died in his own country. He thinks that there must have been two musicians of the name of Dufay. But, until this is cleared up, I will admit the older date, as is yet generally done. Judging from the specimens to which I have had access, of Dufay's works, his harmonies, though correct, sound very often harsh and strange; the movement of the voice-parts is already flowing and melodious. The dissonances are employed with great care and understanding; that is to say, on the unaccented parts of the measures, and as passing notes. Dufay also set secular songs in contrapuntal form. His works

* In F. Chrysander's Jahrbücher für Musikalische Wissenschaft.

are remarkable monuments of the composition of those early times.

The most celebrated contemporaries of Dufay, who distinguished themselves in the same manner of writing, were Egidius Binchois, Vincent Faugues, Eloy, Brassart, Antoine Busnois. These masters all belong to the so-called old school of the Netherlands. But before I speak of the masters of the new school, which commences with Okeghem, and their works, it will be necessary to explain certain technicalities in form, and, at the same time, the meaning of some technical words which are used to designate those forms. An approximative understanding of these forms and technical words will, in a great measure, facilitate a close pursuit of the history of musical art to the amateur, while it will increase his enjoyment.

I have already had occasion to use the expressions "polyphony" and "counterpoint." Polyphony means the union of many parts or voices. The old writers on music always used the word in this sense. The modern theorists use it, however, in a different sense. They apply the term "homophony" to that kind of composition in which the parts move in similar progression and rhythm;

9.

and the term "polyphony" to such compositions as fugues, for instance, in which each of the parts, distinguished by different progression and rhythm, expresses more individual life and melodious flow, although subject to the same laws of harmonious succession. The old contrapuntists, whose only aim was to cultivate this latter form of writing, understood polyphony always in this sense: they thought it superfluous to mark any distinction. This leads us to the word "counterpoint," which signifies point against point; notes being very often called *points* by old writers. Counterpoint — the terror of ignorant superficiality and the object of pretended contempt — has a manifold signification. It would lead me too far to give an explanation here of all its different forms in use in musical writing. I will limit myself to the following. In its broadest sense, to study counterpoint means to study the science of composition in general. In a more limited sense, counterpoint signifies to invent and add to a given part, called *cantus firmus*, one or more parts or melodies. The *cantus firmus* may appear as upper, lower, or middle part. In the works of the old church composers, until the seventeenth century, the *cantus firmus* is always assigned to the voice called *tenor*. The *cantus firmus* was, then, either a Gregorian chant or a people's song (folk-song):

of this latter peculiarity, I shall have an opportunity to speak hereafter. With the ancient church composers, counterpoint meant polyphony in the sense I have explained above.

A contrapuntal form, more or less artificial, is the *canon*. It is a composition in two or more parts, in which the parts, commencing one after the other, imitate each other strictly, note for note: every following part is entirely governed by the construction of the preceding one. Here is a canon from one of Dufay's masses.

10.

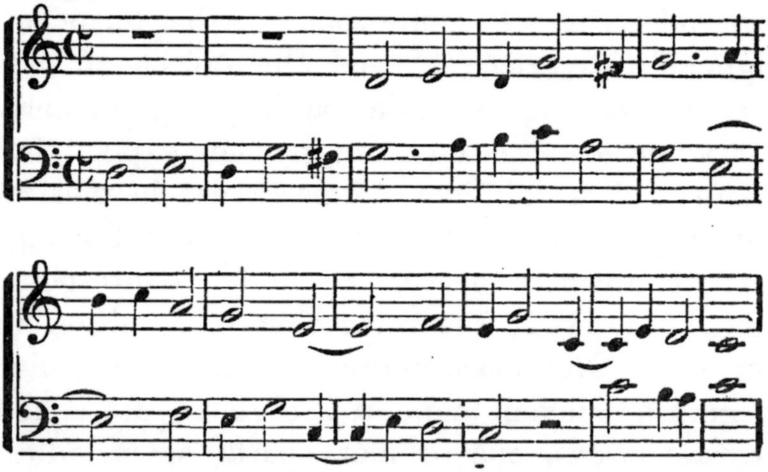

The words *canon* and *fugue*, which are two very distinct forms in our days, were then used to designate the same thing. Canon, as derived from the Greek, means, simply, law or rule. Its application to a fixed form of musical composi tion probably first took place in the following manner. The industrious and ingenious Flemish composers, once started on the path of contrapuntal writing, enriched it step by step, and very often overloaded it, with all kinds of "artificialities:" so much so that these artificialities became proverbial; and subsequent writers on music, and even modern historians, have told us only of the pedantic, dry, and artificial contrapuntal works of the Netherlanders, which seem to be more the productions of arithmetical calculations than those of poetical imagination. This is, however, not entirely the case, as I shall have occasion to prove in speaking of the different masters. It is true that the Flemish composers, masters of polyphonic writing, could not always resist the temptation of making use, perhaps a little too much and too often, of their profound knowledge of counterpoint. So we find that they very often write their fugues, intended for many voices, on one staff, accompanying it with short, often versified devices, to indicate that the composition is not to be sung as it is written, but with certain modifications. The singers of those times, being always learned and accomplished composers, no doubt delighted in those forms. The hint given by the device was called *canon*. *Tinctoris*, a celebrated theorist of the fifteenth century, says, "A canon is a term which indicates the meaning of the composer in a certain obscure way." And another writer, *Hermann Fink*, says, "The canon is a formula, by which the unwritten part of a composition is discovered in the written one." Thus the word canon has been applied to this particular form of composition. The writing of canons became such a mania with some composers of these days, that out of pure habit, or out of ignorance, some even wrote devices indicating a canon, in which no person could discover one. We find canons in augmentation, in diminution, in contrary and backward motion, &c., &c., for two, three, four, and up to thirty parts. Some of them could not be executed at all.

Nevertheless, it was well, that, under the industrious hands of the Flemish composers, the art of constructing works out of one subject, by means of consistent imitation, in which unity of thought and logical form were the prevalent features, should have become established as foundation and principle in all works of a high and lasting merit, till up to our days. Through this they were fitted to become the teachers of other nations: and, when their task was fulfilled, they retired, leaving the field to the Italians, who accomplished, in a more ideal, poetical sense, what the Netherlanders so successfully attempted, and in many respects attained.

John Okeghem (Ockenheim), as stated before, was the principal composer and teacher of the Flemish school, after Dufay, called the new school. The year of his birth and his birthplace are not known with any certainty. Fétis takes the year 1430, Ambros 1415–20. The town of Termond, in East Flanders, is regarded by some musical historians as his birthplace. He began to be celebrated about 1470. In 1476, he became treasurer at the Church of St. Martin, at Tours. After forty years of service under the reign of three French kings, he retired at an advanced age, and died in 1513, at Tours, where he probably passed the last years of his life.

Okeghem was, for a long time, considered the *patriarch of music*, the inventor of the canon, and, in general, of artificial counterpoint. But, as I have already shown, a great and important school preceded him. Okeghem, endowed with great talent, faithfully and industriously cultivated the forms which were in vogue during his time. He brought the canon, however, to very high perfection, and invented many of those often-mentioned contrapuntal artificialities. The voice parts in his compositions, such as masses, motets, and chansons, move with greater freedom: the harmonious treatment possesses still that strange archaic color; however, there is already a breath of tenderness and inward feeling in some portions of these works. Okeghem's influence as a teacher was, perhaps, still greater than as a composer: his reputation spread far and wide, and from all parts of France and Belgium, pupils came to profit by his teachings. The most distinguished of those pupils, who marked the next great epoch of music, were Josquin des Près, Pierre de la Rue, Agricola, Brumel, Gaspard, Loyset Compère, Verbonnet. The art of writing those artificial canons, before mentioned, was much cultivated at this epoch. The most celebrated contemporaries of Okeghem were the Netherlanders, John Regis, Firmain Caron, Busnoys, Jacob Hobrecht, who is spoken of as a very fine composer (Glarean says, "He had so much invention, that he could compose a whole mass in one night"). Hobrecht was also the teacher in music of the celebrated Erasmus of Rotterdam. Also the renowned theorists and writers on music, John Tinctoris, William Guarnerie, Bernardus Hycaert, lived in Okeghem's time.

I have already mentioned that the old church composers very often used secular songs and folk-songs as *cantus firmus* in their masses and motets, besides the Gregorian chant,—a practice which was in use until the seventeenth century. It has been proven by such writers as Fétis, Coussemaker, Nizard and Ambros, that this was a custom which the first Flemish contrapuntists received from their neighbors, the French. That musical art among the Netherlanders sprang up at once, as an isolated fact, is, of course, not the case; and the recently discovered specimens of old masses, chansons, and other pieces, by early French composers, has shown who were the masters of the first Flemish composers. But France, under the misrule of weak and frivolous kings, had then to celebrate tournaments, and to make wars: there was no time for the development and cultivation of peaceful arts. The Low Countries, a part of which was under the government of the dukes of Burgundy, were thus in immediate social and commercial relations with France. From there they received, no doubt, the first impulse to the cultivation of musical art, and with it the habit of taking secular melodies, as well as Gregorian chants, as tenor, or *cantus firmus* in their works for the Church. And, as the social and political situation of the people was then entirely influenced by the Church, the boundaries of profane and secular music were less distinctly divided than at a later period. Thus, from the first masses of any artistic merit by William Dufay, which are composed over the melodies, entitled, "*Se la face ay pâle*," "*Tant je me deduis*," "*L'homme armé*," &c., until Palestrina, we find masses written over profane *chansons;* for instance, "*Adieu, mes amours,*" "*Malheur me bat,*" "*Des rouges nez,*" &c., &c. But the most used as tenor was "*L'homme armé.*" Every composer, from Dufay to Palestrina (and even Carissimi himself), has written masses on this melody, over and over again. Every thing sanctioned by habit being, in the course of time, admitted as essential, the composers of all this period in our musical art never dreamed of, or intended, any thing contrary to the dignity of the Church. Moreover, most of the composers, in their qualities of singers and chapel masters, were priests. The masses of a composer were then distinguished by the title of the melodies of the tenor; and it sounds curious to read the mass of "The Red Noses," or that of "Farewell, my Love," that of "The Armed Man," that of "He has a pale Face," &c., &c. Masses, which were not composed over such a tenor, were simply termed masses *sine nomine.* Many voices were loud against this custom, and condemned it as a profanation of divine service: others defended it. But in the course of time, probably not without being much abused by composers, this method of writing disappeared entirely. Through more experience and richer invention, aided by continual practice in the difficult art of counterpoint, composers could rely more on themselves.

and stand upon their own feet, needing no longer the help of the leading-strings of those early and *naïve* composers for the church.

The greatest composer of the third epoch of the Netherlanders, and, in fact, the first who created works which still possess artistic merit, was *Josquin des Près* (Jodocus Pratensis). Josquin was born, probably, in 1445, and probably, also, in Condé, but we know certainly in Hainault. A singular fate persecuted our greatest masters: we very often do not know where they came from. Like a comet, they appear, shine, and disappear, and we are very often uncertain when and where. Their real existence, their real characters, are too often obscured by a store of absurd, untrue, worthless anecdotes of their lives. They are only too often represented as jesters dealing in silly jokes, which are recounted with minute details, and especially if they possess a vein of humor, under which the grandeur of their characters, the powerful and lofty aspirations of their minds, the richness and sublimity of their imaginations, are buried. Dry theorists and superficial critics, with their multiplication and division tables continually at hand, cannot understand or appreciate genius when it does not accord with *their* figures. So it was with Josquin, the first real great musical genius who marks an era in our musical art: so it was with Mozart, the last great universal musical genius who appeared. Even Beethoven and Schubert could not escape the same false representations.

But to return to Josquin. After he had finished his studies with Okeghem, he must have directed his steps towards Rome; for under the pontificate of Sixtus IV., from 1471 to 1484, we find him as a singer in the pope's chapel. The reason which prompted him to leave such an honorable position is not known. Was it, that, like all great geniuses, he was persecuted by envy and jealousy before he found recognition? After leaving the service of the pope, Josquin des Près remained for some time in Florence, and also in Ferrara, in Italy, where at last he found recognition, and where his genius, in continual contact with art and art-loving men, must have received the deepest impression. Josquin returned to his own country, and about 1498 we meet him at the court of Louis XII. of France. It cannot be ascertained for how long a time he remained at the court of France. He is said to have been in the service of the Emperor Maximilian, which is probably an error. Josquin died at Condé, Aug. 27, 1521.

So great was Josquin's reputation as a composer, while living, that his works were preferred to those of all others: his name was sufficient to stamp a work as excellent. A motet by Adrian Willaert, "*Verbum bonum est*," for six voices, was sung for a long time in the Sixtine Chapel, and was supposed to be a composition of Josquin's. Willaert, who happened to come to Rome, where he heard the motet performed, of course claimed it as *his* work. But the prejudice of the singers was so great, that they refused to sing the motet any longer. Castiglione also relates a similar fact: "A motet, sung before the Duchess of Urbino, was totally disregarded, till known to have come from the pen of Josquin, when it excited universal extasy." Does not this remind us of many a similar case in our days? For want of sound and just appreciation and judgment in an audience, fine and original works are too often only indorsed when the composer's name has already acquired the prestige of a certain reputation among connoisseurs. Andrea Adami calls Josquin the brightest luminary in the heaven of music, from whom all composers who succeeded him had to learn. So all his contemporaries constantly eulogized his learning and his genius. Luther was very fond of Josquin's music. After having heard one of his motets performed, he exclaimed, "Josquin is a master of the notes: they had to do as *he* pleased, while they made other composers do as *they* pleased."

Josquin, like every great composer that has appeared until our days, was very industrious, and paid, in many of his works, a tribute to the taste of his time; but he created many, which, if only known, will still excite the admiration of the connoisseur, and especially his motets and psalms. It was not until after years of minute polishing, that Josquin allowed his works to be made public, although he mastered all the intricacies of the most artificial contrapuntal art with the greatest ease and facility. "When we consider," says Commer very justly, "that Josquin's predecessors were merely men who regarded the artificial construction of contrapuntal phrases as of the highest consequence; when we reflect, that, in his motets, he broke through earlier boundaries, and sought, with all his contrapuntal art, to give full signification to the meaning of the words, — we are astonished at what he accomplished, and forced to unite with his contemporaries in their admiration for him. Josquin not only stands above those composers who lived before and with him; not only above a great number of those who succeeded him, — but his motets are such master-works, that, well-performed, they will be listened to, through all time, as real jewels among sacred compositions."

The epoch of Josquin des Près is already rich in celebrated composers; and the progress of music, since the time of Dufay, is astonishing. Not alone composers, but theorists of great merit and profound knowledge, endeavored to explain and systematize the methods which led on Okeghem, Josquin des Près, and others, in the production of their works, and in their teachings. The most celebrated of Josquin's pupils were Certon, Clement Jannequin, Maillard, Moulu, Claudin Sermisy, Jean Mouton, Adrien Petit (called Coclicus), Arcadelt, Bourgogne, Nicolas Gombert, Jaquet von Berghem.

The invention of printing notes with movable metal types, in the year 1502, was of the greatest influence on the development of musical art. The inventor's name was *Ottavio Petrucci da Fossombrone*, in Italy. Through Petrucci's invention, the printing of musical works became cheaper than the old indistinct prints with wooden types; and the enterprising Petrucci published, in quick succession, selections of masses, motets, chansons, and other works, by the favorite composers of this time. Petrucci's invention soon found its way to other cities and countries. German printers, especially, availed themselves of it very soon, and busily printed and reprinted, for the music-loving public, new and recognized works of different composers.

Thus we see musical art, after centuries of

struggle and labor, arrived at that point where composers and theorists, aided by successful and industrious printers, who facilitated the knowledge of their works, worked together, hand in hand, to reveal to the human mind the existence of the not less wonderful creations of man's imagination.

With the exception of a few German and French composers, Dutch masters had the universal control of musical matters in nearly all the European chapels and church choirs of any consequence. In the next and fourth period, called the epoch of Willaert, the school of the Netherlanders reached its zenith; after which, other masters, Italians, stepped in, and obtained the supremacy which had been so long and so ably held by the Netherlanders.

Adrian Willaert, born at Bruges, in Flanders, in the year 1490, is said to have been a pupil of Jean Mouton, possibly, also, of Josquin des Près himself. He first studied law at the University of Paris, which, however, he soon abandoned for the study of music. As a young man of twenty-six, he had already made himself a name with his compositions in his own country. In 1518, he went to Rome. But it seems he was not successful in endeavoring to procure himself a position in Rome: he went, therefore, to try his luck in Venice. He succeeded so well there, that, in 1527, he had already obtained the position of a maestro in the Church of St. Marc, a position which was considered in Venice that of a musical dignitary. Willaert's influence, as a composer and teacher of musical science and art, was great and beneficial. He was the founder of the celebrated Venetian school of music, from which sprang so many distinguished composers, theorists, and singers. Willaert is also the father of the madrigal, a form of which I will speak hereafter. He introduced the double chorus in the antiphonal form. Willaert died the 7th of December, 1562. The most celebrated of his pupils were Cyprian de Rore (who was his successor, and to whom the Italians gave the title of "Il divino)," whose works may be counted as of the best among those of his contemporaries; and also the distinguished theorist Zarlino, Constanzo Porta, Nicolo Vincento, Della Viola. Flemish masters, who lived and distinguished themselves at this fourth and last epoch of the Netherlanders, were Christian and Sebastian Hollander, Thomas Crequillon, Jacobus de Kerle, Orlandus Lassus, Clemens non Papa, Matthieu Le Maistre, Andreas Pevernage, Jacobus Vaet, Coradius Verdonk, Hubertus Walrant, and many others.

Arrived at the turning-point of musical culture among the Netherlanders, I will next proceed to pass in brief review the labors of the other European nations in the field of musical composition during all this period.

From the earliest times, music, vocal and instrumental, was pursued with great application and talent in England; and, in the development of harmony and counterpoint, it had an equal share with other European nations. An old author, Tinctoris, and with him many ancient and modern writers, are even inclined to attribute to the English the honor of being the inventors of counterpoint; and *Dunstable*, about 1420, was, in his time, considered the foremost among English composers. Though their neighbors, the French and Dutch musicians, became masters of the situation, the English also made considerable progress in that art; and composers like Robert Fairfax, John Digon, John Shepard, John Marbeck, John Tavern, John Parsons, Christopher Tye, Robert White, and many others, contributed not a little towards the most brilliant epoch of musical art in England, headed by Thomas Tallis, his great pupil Bird, Morley (a pupil of Bird), Dowland, Weelkes, John Bull, John Wilbye, Orlando Gibbons, &c. Though many a fine motet and anthem owes its origin to these composers, their madrigals are yet more interesting, more original, more beautiful, and more fresh. The madrigal was then the favorite form of English composers. Besides the compositions which belong to, and also make an essential part of, the service of the church, such as masses, motets, psalms, hymns, &c., composers, from the earliest dates at which music was written in different parts, were very industrious in composing to secular words, melodies and part songs for the wants of musical amateurs. And in different countries, according to the peculiarities of the people, these songs, the deeper expression of individual life, took different forms in melodious construction as well as in harmonious treatment. Thus in France we find the *chanson*, in Germany the *Lied*, in England the *song* and the *glee*, in Italy the *frottole*, the *villote*, the *canzonet.* I will here only treat of the madrigal.

"*Madrigal* (Webster's definition) is a word derived from *mandra*, or *mandria*, a flock, a sheep-fold, a herd of cattle: hence madrigal, originally a pastoral song; a little, amorous poem, containing some tender and delicate, though simple thought." We already know that composers have selected for their masses, very often, Gregorian chants or secular melodies for tenor. In the madrigal, the composition rested upon original invention, thus allowing more variety in form and contrapuntal treatment. In the madrigal, the composer's endeavor was to express, through adequate music, the meaning of the poem: he followed closely, with appropriate motives, the sentiment of the different verses. Strict and elaborate canons and fugues were thus out of place in the madrigal; and, though seemingly simple in its construction, the composer found ample opportunity to display his mastery in contrapuntal writing. Great variety in rhythm, poetical expression, characteristic melodies, new and striking harmonies, were considered as the necessary qualities of the madrigal. It was generally set for three, four, five, six, and even more parts, though writing in five parts seems to have been most in favor and use. I have already mentioned that Adrian Willaert is considered, if not as its inventor, at any rate, as the composer who gave it its first artistic form. The madrigal may be considered as the highest form of chamber-music in those days, written and composed for the refined and appreciative amateurs of the best social circles, principally in Venice and Rome. All composers of any name produced works in this favorite form: among others, I will mention, besides Willaert, Cyprian de Rore, Constanzo Porta, Constanzo Festa, Verdelot, Arcadelt, Palestrina, Orlandus Lassus, Orazio Vecchi, the Prince of Venossa, and Luca Marenzio, the madrigalist *par excellence*.

The madrigal, after its first introduction from

Italy into England, about 1583, flourished especially there; and such composers as Dowland, Weelkes, Morley, Cobbold, Farmer, and many others, have created works, which, through their freshness and exquisite charm in melodious, harmonic, and contrapuntal treatment, will, when well performed, still receive the admiration of musicians and amateurs. "The charming, and, in a certain sense, unequalled madrigals of these masters differ essentially from those of the Italians and Netherlanders. It is well known, that the British Islands (England, Ireland, and Scotland) possess a large number of folk-songs of the most wonderful beauty. The madrigals are either founded on these folk-songs, or, in melodic invention, they imitate them throughout; while the masterly texture of the voice-parts just touches on the boundaries of that hair-line where melody still remains true to itself, and yet is moved by the rich life of polyphony. There can be nothing more graceful than a few of the pieces of Dowland and Morley. They are at once naïvely folk-like and simple, yet really courteous. It is society music in the best sense, and music which may thank society of the times of Elizabeth — society that was rich in strong and handsome women, and chivalric, pure men — for its rise and development. It is, indeed, one of the most pleasing flowers of that Elizabethan soil." *

In 1601, Thomas Morley published a selection of madrigals, to which twenty different composers contributed. The collection is called the "Triumph of Oriana:" the motto of each madrigal was "Long live fair Oriana;" and, in the fair Oriana, Queen Elizabeth was honored.

It would lead me too far to speak of the different changes the madrigal was subject to in the course of time. In my account of the musical drama, — the opera and the oratorio, — however, we shall meet it again. Suffice it here to say, that, in its musical construction, it greatly influenced the forms of other compositions, and especially of the motet.

In Germany, the progress of musical development, so peculiar and natural to its people, was pursued steadfastly and consistently from its earliest state, until it became, in our modern times, the head of a school. Of the distinguished German composers, who were perfect masters of all the different forms of counterpoint, and who created works unsurpassed by any of the Dutch composers, I must mention *Henry Fink*, who flourished about 1480; *Henry Isaac* (born about 1440), called by the Italians *Arrigo Tedesco*, one of the greatest among composers.

* Ambros: Geschichte der Musik

His masses, motets, and German part-songs may be counted among the finest works produced at this time. Other renowned composers were Stephen Mahu, Lorenz Lemlin, Sixt Dietrich, Arnold von Bruck, Ludwig Senfle, a pupil of Isaac, and, perhaps, no less a great composer than his master Isaac. Luther was especially fond of Senfle's motets. Besides masses and motets, he has composed admirable part-songs to German words. Of other German composers, I shall speak more elaborately in the lecture on the Oratorio; and especially of those who played so conspicuous a part at the time of the Reformation, and who adorned the rising Protestant (Lutheran) Church with many noble sacred hymns, which were the germs of a new and vigorous form of Protestant church-music.

Spain furnished, in the sixteenth century, some excellent singers and composers to the pope's chapel in Rome; and, to judge from the works of these masters, one cannot help wondering that musical culture of a higher order, with few and rare exceptions, was, at a later period, so entirely neglected by a nation which has given proof of so much, so exquisite, so truly poetic, talent for that art. We may consider *Cristofano Morales* as the representative of Spanish composers. This great master was born at the beginning of the sixteenth century. In 1540, under

Pope Paul III., he was admitted as a singer in the Sixtine Chapel. Morales points already, in many of his works, to the noble and pure church style of Palestrina. Morales was an upright, thorough, and honest artist. His serious and noble character, true to his Spanish nationality, can be distinguished in the following lines, which form a part of his preface to a book of masses: "I despise," he says, "all superficial, frivolous music, and never occupied myself with it. The object of music is to strengthen and ennoble the soul. If it does else save honor God, and illustrate the thoughts and feelings of great men, it entirely misses its aim. But what shall I say of those men, who, gifted with divine power of creating music, misuse their power in a contemptible manner? There are such men, however, on whose ingratitude it is impossible to look without indignation. And their works alone are those that deserve the epithets, enervating, demoralizing. But, should any one pretend to say that *all music* is a frivolous luxury, he may rest assured that the frivolity, and other defects besides, are to be looked for in *his own breast*, and not in the nature of music." Among other Spanish composers, I will mention Escobedo, Scribano, the two Guerros, Soto, Ortiz, and, before all, the admirable Vittoria.

It is difficult to draw a line of demarcation

between the styles of French and Flemish composers of this time. The southern provinces of the Low Countries being populated by a people entirely of the same race as the French, the only difference was that of residence in another country. Until our days, many of the Dutch composers were even classified with the French: from this we find the school of the Netherlanders, also often called *Gallo-Belgian.* Only one of the French masters (and he is too often called a Flemish composer) will occupy our attention here, who, through his influence as the founder of the great Roman school of music, and, as such, the master of Palestrina, and also through his charming compositions, prepared the epoch in which real Catholic church music reached its purest and most idealistic forms; and that artist was *Claude Goudimel.* Goudimel was born at Vaison, near Avignon, at the beginning of the sixteenth century; and, on suspicion of being a Huguenot, the 24th of August, 1572, on that terrible night of the massacre of French Protestants, called St. Bartholomew's Night, he was killed at Lyons, and his corpse thrown into the Rhone. Goudimel has written masses and motets of exquisite tenderness, of rare charm, of remarkable clearness in form, — qualities of which his great pupil, Palestrina, made so effective a use. Of his arrangement of the Psalms of David, translated into French by Clement Marot and Theodore de Bèze, I shall speak in my lecture on the Oratorio. The distinguished composers, Animuccia, Bettini, Nanino, Merlo, called Della Viola, were, besides Palestrina, pupils of Goudimel. Other French composers at this time were Pierre Certon, Clement Jannequin, Phinot, Claude le Jeune, Carpentras.

The Italians, under the guidance of such excellent composers and teachers as the Netherlanders, made themselves gradually masters of the difficult art of counterpoint. It was not in the nature of the Italians to express themselves in such complicated forms as counterpoint presents. Counterpoint, as I have already proved, is the production of the Northern *German* mind: and, like the Gothic style of architecture, each part of the complicated form is only understood in connection with the whole composition; and, though every one of these parts is brought to the greatest individual perfection, they all concur in the expression of one great thought, of one great idea. Like all Gothic art, this form reflects, in its variety of rhythm, in its richness of harmony, and its finish and perfection of workmanship, the social and political situation of the Northern nations in the middle ages, till up to the "Renaissance," and, at the same time, the dreamy and fanciful imagination of these nations. Not outward, like the Italian, but within itself, rests the ideal of the German artist; and, in his endeavor to give expression to his deep and soul-felt thoughts, he not seldom creates works overladen with contrapuntal details, obscured by richness of harmony, often incomprehensible for want of clear, formal construction, and which only such gigantic minds as J. S. Bach and Beethoven could triumphantly overcome. In Italy, pure Gothic architecture and essentially Gothic arts never could take root. Surrounded by the classic remains of old Greek and Roman art, influenced by the beautiful, serene, and warm climate, the peculiarity of their nature is more inclined to outward expression in clear, simple, but grandiose forms. There is a repose and a quieting influence in their whole art, a reflex of the lovely lines, the beautiful sky, which overhangs the charming Italian landscape. The whole existence of the Italians is an outward one, which, at the same time, points to superficiality, to empty and cold formalism. And this is not so perceivable in any branch of their art as in music. Hence the dissonance between German and Italian art. When these two characteristic qualities, which distinguish the Italian from the German mind, are found combined, though very rarely, in such individualities as Palestrina, Orlandus Lassus,

Handel, and Mozart, then art reaches that point of universal excellence which makes its works the æsthetical expression of no single nationality, of no single individuality, but of the spirit of the whole age; and they are accepted as lasting and ideal forms of artistic enjoyment for all men and for all times, and as lofty monuments of man's mind and imagination, exceptionally gifted by the fructifying and creative finger of God.

Constanzo Festa is considered as the first Italian composer who became a thorough master in counterpoint. He was admitted as a singer in the Sixtine Chapel in 1517, and died 1245, much beloved, and much esteemed as a composer during his life. Though Festa's works everywhere give proof of his having been a pupil of the school of the Netherlanders, yet they already display much of that tenderness, purity, and chaste simplicity, which distinguished the works of the great Italian composers who followed him. Baini asserts that Palestrina studied Festa's works closely; nay, he considers Festa as the immediate predecessor, the model composer, in that noble style of church music which stamps the works of Palestrina as unique in form and idea.

Giovanni Pierluigi, called *Palestrina* from the name of his birthplace, was born, according to

Baini, his biographer, in the year 1524. Kandler, the German translator of Baini's work, on the strength of an inscription on an old portrait of Palestrina which exists in the archives of the singers in the Sixtine Chapel, was inclined to take 1514 as the year of his birth. It has been proved quite recently, however, that Kandler was right in fixing 1514. E. Schelle, on a visit to Rome, had the good fortune to examine the family papers and other documents formerly belonging to our master, which were discovered by Cicerchio, a pupil of Baini, among the archives of the town of Palestrina, near Rome. Baini, so enthusiastic in his admiration of Palestrina, so exclusive in his favorable judgment of his hero's works whenever he has to reward the merit of others also, never took the trouble of journeying to the near birthplace of the master. He preferred to give us very learned and elaborate speculations, founded on anecdotes and bulls of the pope, &c., and to admit the wrong date, when, by a half-a-day's journey, he would have been able to state the right one. Schelle also tells us that Palestrina's family-name was *Sante;* that the master's parents, though not rich, were yet well off, and able to give their son good instruction. It is very touchingly stated, in some books, that Palestrina, as a poor peasant-boy, came to Rome; that his great musical talent was then discovered; and that, through all kinds of privations and adventures, he became a celebrated composer. It is, however, as I have stated before, not true. Palestrina received his first musical instruction in his own city, where he was also for some time organist at the cathedral. He afterwards went to Rome, where he obtained his first engagement as a teacher of the choir-boys of St. Peter's, in the Vatican, in the year 1551, and was subsequently chapel-master there. In 1554, he published his first book of masses for four and five parts, and was, in 1555, admitted in the Sixtine Chapel; but, as he was married, Pope Paul IV., who considered it contrary to the rule of his chapel, which excludes laymen, had him dismissed. But in latter years, his reputation as a composer of church music having become great, Pope Pius IV., wishing to have him back, created, expressly for him, the position of "Composer to the pope's chapel," a distinction, which, after Palestrina's death, was conferred only on one more composer, Felix Anerio. Palestrina died in the year 1594.

Palestrina, like every great composer, closely and diligently studied the works of his predecessors. Formed in that great school of the Netherlanders, he faithfully followed its principles and traditions; and in many of his works he paid a tribute to that school. Though very often considered as the reformer of true church music, it was not in outward formal endeavors that he perfected the organism of his art, but by ennobling, enriching, purifying its inward contents; by idealizing, in the sense of the Catholic Church, its mystic religious life. Palestrina's genius, so rich, so fruitful, attained its truest and grandest expression in the musical embodiment of the rites of his Church. Perhaps more than any other composer, he found those sympathetic yet heavenly-pure touches, which enabled him to lend adequate musical expression to that rich liturgy, so dear to the Catholic Christian. In Palestrina's works, Catholic church music found its greatest and purest revelation: they mark the culminating point, and at the same time, I may say, the close, of a great and unique epoch in our musical art.

Palestrina founded his style, which was called after him the *Palestrina style*, upon the study of Gregorian chant in its purest meaning: from that source he drew his wonderful inspiration. No master studied Gregorian chant more deeply than Palestrina: no one, before or after, knew better how to use it with more artistic variety and success. Palestrina remained true, all his life, to the traditions of the system of the ecclesiastical modes. He was a stranger to the nervous striving of some of his contemporaries for new and striking harmonious means with which to enrich their works, and which resulted, finally, in the overthrow of the system of the ecclesiastical keys, and the substitution of our modern tonalities (major and minor keys) instead, which rest upon the tonic and dominant.

Palestrina had the good fortune, while yet living, to see his merit recognized. He was very industrious all his life, and has composed a vast number of works.

I have yet to mention one great event in Palestrina's life. Nearly all writers on the history of music make it of great importance, embellishing it, according to the force of their own imaginations, with more or less romantic colors. It is this: At the Council of Trent, in the year 1562, among other reforms which concerned the service of the Catholic Church and its government, the question of a reform of church music was also agitated. We are told that the reverend fathers, at this time, were very much incensed about the frivolity with which composers introduced profane melodies as the fundamental theme, the tenor, in their masses and other compositions, and the contrapuntal artificialities with which works destined for the edification of church service were overloaded, — so much so, that the words could not be understood ; and that, but for the genius of Palestrina, figurated or contrapuntal music would have been banished from the Catholic Church for all times. Pope Pius IV., before taking sweeping measures, appointed a committee of cardinals, and singers of his chapel, to examine the subject, and to recommend means for a necessary reform. Palestrina, already known by some exquisite works, at the request of the committee produced three masses, of which one, in six parts, pleased throughout, and received the admiration of every one. It is the celebrated "*Missa Papæ Marcelli*," which Palestrina dedicated, in grateful remembrance, to his former protector, the Pope Marcellus II. Since this time, we are accustomed to see Palestrina called the *Saviour of church music.*

Of course this mass is a wonderful work throughout ; but as to that simplicity in contrapuntal treatment, which, according to most writers on the subject, makes this mass so different from the works of other composers of this time, I could never discover it. Artificial contrapuntal form predominates from the first number "Kyrie eleison," — which is built upon a canon, — to the end. Baini, the most prolific source of these reports, thinks it, of course, necessary for the glory of his hero to raise him, Atlas-like, above all other composers; and, to dissipate all doubts, he discourages students, through unjust and severe judgment, from referring to the master-works of Palestrina's predecessors and contemporaries. That the genius of Palestrina created a work in the old traditional forms, which, through its great beauties, disarmed the enemies of counterpoint, — where, perhaps, lies the whole question of a reform in church music, — shows the invariable truth which rests at the foundation of the art-principle of those Netherlanders, — an art-principle, the very germ of our modern music, and one that will hold good for all time. But to admit, as Baini would have us, that, because Palestrina is so great, with very few exceptions the works of other composers who lived before and with him are inferior productions, full of dry, contrapuntal artificialities, without meaning, without invention, &c., &c., is simply a great injustice to those worthy masters. Any one, who, without prejudice, knows how to read, and has the faculty of correctly judging what he hears, will soon be convinced of the narrowness of the views and judgments of Baini, Burney, and others, in regard to most of the works, principally the beautiful motets, of such masters as Josquin des Près, Arcadelt, Clemens non Papa, Morales, Cyprian de Rore,

Orlando di Lasso, Willaert, Festa, and a host of others. Though full of the highest admiration for the great and exceptional genius of Palestrina, yet this does not exclude my appreciation, my veneration, for the noble works of the Flemish, German, and French composers of this remarkable epoch in our musical art. And, feeling the beauties of the works of these masters, I never could understand yet how church music then needed a saviour. Can it be, that then, as in our own days, singers and organists ignored the noble works of the truly great and inspired masters, and substituted, in their stead, the shallow, insipid, frivolous productions of mercenary art? for, in musical art, it is unfortunately only too often the case, that superficial knowledge and deficient judgment and talent usurp the claims of real merit, real knowledge, real talent.

The genius of the Netherlanders, which, for nearly two centuries, stood at the head of musical culture in Europe, at the close of its mission seemed once more to concentrate all its power, all its peculiarity, all its fertility, on one master, the greatest of all his nation, inferior to none of his contemporaries, — *Orlandus Lassus*, or *Orlando di Lasso.*

Orlandus Lassus was born at Mons, in Haiuault, in 1520. In his youth, he was a choir-boy at the St. Nicolas Cathedral, in his native city, and, if the anecdote be truly told, was kidnapped not less than three times on account of his fine voice. At the age of twelve years, he accompanied Ferdinand de Gonsaga to Milan. He afterwards went to Rome; and, at the age of twenty-one, he was already chapel-master at the Basilica St. Giovanni in Laterano. In 1557, he received an engagement in the chapel of Albert V., at Munich, where he remained until his death, which occurred the 15th of June, 1594.

The mind of Lassus was, perhaps, more productive than that of any other composer. It is estimated that he composed the immense number of two thousand works! A modern writer, Carlus Proske, gives so just an estimate of Lassus' great genius, that I cannot do better than to insert it here. "Orlando di Lasso possessed a universal mind. No one among his contemporaries had such a clear will, or such a mastery over the machinery of his art: whatever he needed for his tone-picture, he was able to grasp with certainty. He was never unsuccessful, whether in the contemplative mood of the church, or in the merry caprices of profane song. He was great both in the lyric and epic styles, and would have been still greater in the dramatic, had his age possessed this branch of musical composition. In his works, we discover traits of such dramatic, epic truth and strength, that we feel as if we had been fanned by the breath of a Dante, a Michael Angelo. If we place Palestrina by the side of Raffaelle, it will not be too far-fetched a comparison to place our master beside the great Florentine. Lassus united in himself so much that was to be found at that time in the music of each European nation, that he appeared unique, as well as characteristic, and could not be held up as an especially Italian, German, Belgian, or French composer. No one resembled him in this peculiarity more than the great Handel; and as he united in himself the German, Italian, and English genius of the eighteenth century, so in the works of Lassus we find the combined glories of German and Roman art of his time."

Although many of Lassus' works were easily accessible to Baini and Burney, yet these, in many regards meritorious writers, were blinded as to the great merit of these works. Burney, in his "General History of Music," says, "Indeed, the compositions *a capella* of Cyprian Rore and Orlando Lasso are much inferior to those of Palestrina, in this peculiarity: for, by striving to be grave and solemn, they only become heavy and dull; and what is unaffected dignity in the Roman is little better than the strut of a dwarf upon stilts in the Netherlanders." Baini in his "*Memorie Storico-critiche*" of Palestrina, mentions Lassus in the following terms: "Orlandus Lassus, a Netherlander by birth and in his art, without fine ideas, without life and spirit; a man, who, through the composition of a *few* (?) masses and motets in a simple style, and in eight parts, has usurped the exaggerated praise, — *Lassus, lassum qui recreat orbem.*" This is a part of Lassus' epitaph, which, by a play on the name of Lassus, signifies, "Here rests the weary who refreshed the weary." It has been reserved to our time, however, to set the works of Lassus, and of many other unjustly forgotten masters, in the right light.

With Orlandus Lassus' death, sacred musical art in the Low Countries vanished, as by enchantment, while in Italy it flourished in a new and brighter light. Such composers as Anerio, the Spaniard Vittoria, Suriano, Luca Marenzio, the two Gabrieli, Monteverde, Carissimi, Alessandro Scarlatti, &c., created works after works, which were everywhere greeted with delight, and which gave the Italians that prestige in musical matters which they retained, all over Europe, until the beginning of the present century.

THIRD LECTURE.

The Oratorio, including the Passion, the Mystery and Miracle Plays, and Protestant Church Music from the Twelfth Century to the Death of Schumann.

Our modern oratorio and opera both took root in, and trace their origin from, those early sacred plays called Mysteries, Moralities, or Miracle Plays. Those Eastern nations, the descendants of the Greeks and the Romans, after their conversion to the Christian religion, would persist, so history tells us, in their natural tendency to theatrical representations, — a remnant of the old heathen practice, as well in religious as in secular life; and the subjects of these theatrical representations, in spite of anathemas from the pulpit, were almost solely taken from heathen mythology. But, in the first centuries of the Christian religion, it was soon apparent to the heads of the new Church, that to impress the lively imaginations of these nations, and to attract them to the service of the new religion, it was necessary to give their religious service symbolic forms in order to reach the mind through the senses. In the new religion, they were to find every thing more beautiful than in the old. With this many a heathen custom first found its way into the ceremonies of the new Church, and also the love for theatrical representations. Thus we find, from the earliest times, among all nations, the dramatic element, so innate to man's nature, first associated with religious worship. With the dominion of the Christian religion all over Europe, and in the similarity of the arrangement of the religious office, the same customs, the same ceremonies, established themselves in the different churches. The priests, the supreme guides of the congregation in spiritual and social matters, — even, to a certain degree, in politics also, — were eager to turn all their tendencies to secular festivities and amusements to the benefit of the Church, and, to this end, arranged spiritual plays, the subjects taken from the Old and New Testaments, or the lives of the saints, &c., which were played, for instruction and edification in the religious mysteries, on a stage erected in the building of the church, generally under the choir. Priests in appropriate costumes, representing, according to the subject, God the Father, Christ, the angels, and Mary, were the actors; and, as women were not allowed to appear on the stage, their parts were also in the hands of priests. That these sacred representations made a great impression upon the pious audiences can be proved by many an historical fact. It is said, that, at the miracle play of the five wise and five foolish virgins, acted in the year 1322, before the elector Frederic, at Eisenach, a scene representing the five foolish virgins, who vainly besought, with great fervor, the Virgin Mary and the saints for their intercession at the throne of God, and for admission into Paradise, excited the elector so much, that he exclaimed, with great indignation, "To what good are Christianity and pious works, if even the prayers of the saints cannot procure help and forgiveness?" He was so deeply moved, that he had a stroke of apoplexy, of which he afterwards died. In the course of the next centuries, profane elements, principally in Italy, Spain, and France, where the traditions of the old Roman theatrical representations were not yet entirely extinguished, began to be mixed with the holy legends. As these miracle and mystery plays became more and more the favorite entertainments of the congregations, they lasted several days, and the number of actors amounted to several hundreds. Soon the churches were not ample enough to give room to the eager audiences; and thus immense stages were erected in the streets, on market-places, and even in cemeteries. These stages, built of boards, were generally divided into three stories. The upper one represented heaven, the second earth, and the lowest hell. The actors marched in procession to their different places. Corporations formed themselves to arrange the miracle plays in a more regular way. In Rome, the "Compagnia del Confalone" existed (in the latter part of the thirteenth century), which selected the Coliseum for its place of meeting. In Paris, we see the "Confrèrie de la Passion," the "Confrèrie de Bazoche." As soon as these mystery and miracle plays passed from the hands of the priests and monks into those of the people, their character of sacred representations lost its dignity and meaning. Jongleurs, histrions, and all sorts of vagabonds, took a lively part in these plays; and thus the sacred elements were not seldom submerged by profane satires, comic scenes, and gross buffoonery. Therefore it is not strange that these people began to rival each other in obscene deeds and language: the most holy rites of religious ceremonies were degraded by low and silly jokes; instead of sacred hymns, impudent street-songs resounded before the altar of the church; and the most important person in the miracle plays, though also the most abused, was the devil. He was very popular with our forefathers. They dressed him up in the most fantastic, extravagant, and alarming manner. In France, not less than four devils had sometimes to appear in one play. He did not yet represent the bad principle; but his parts were those of a clown, or a poor, abused imbecile. He always got the worst of it. "All Fools' Day" and the "Donkey's Festival" were, for a long time, the most popular occasion of general amusement. At the "Donkey's Festival," in commemoration of the flight of Mary with the infant Christ to Egypt, a donkey was dressed in the gown of a monk, and thus led into the church: sometimes a young girl, holding a doll, to represent Mary with the child, rode on it. Then the priest intoned the Latin hymn, "Orientis partibus." The congregation responded by repeating the last verse, "Hez, Sir Ane, hez."*

11.

During the whole ridiculous ceremony, psalms and hymns, parodied by the most absurd versions, were sung, intermixed with the imitation of the brayings of the donkey. "All Fools' Day," a tradition of the old Roman Sa-

* Forkel: Geschichte der Music.

turnalia, was celebrated in just as grotesque a manner. Though the humor of our ancestors very often lost all control of itself in the celebration of the miracle-plays, from the element of these mysteries and moralities, as I have said before, emerged the forms of the oratorio and the opera, the richest, and, in an artistic as well as in a poetical sense, the highest, of modern musical art-forms.

The origin of the name "Oratorio," applied to a particular art-form, is the following: Those great reforms in the Christian Church, inaugurated at the beginning of the sixteenth century by Luther in Germany, and long ago felt and hoped for, as inevitably necessary, by the purest and noblest minds, could not fail to affect and influence, in the most salutary way, the whole Catholic world. Among those of the Catholic clergy who deeply deplored the great demoralization which then menaced the overthrow of the old religion, who at the same time saw the necessity of a return to purer, more legitimate Christian principles, and who devoted the most precious hours of their life to these purposes, appears *St. Philip Neri*, born 1515, in Florence, and in 1561 consecrated as a priest at Rome. Neri afterwards founded a congregation of priests in Rome. Before these congregations, he explained biblical histories; and, in order to draw youths to church, and to keep them from secular amusements, he used to have hymns, psalms, and other "Laudi spirituali," or spiritual songs, sung alternately with his teachings. But, to render these pious meetings still more attractive, he arranged and dramatized, in a simple form, the sacred stories or events from the Scriptures, such as "The Good Samaritan," "Job and his Friends," "The Prodigal Son," "Tobias and the Angels," &c. These pieces were written in verse, and set to music in the manner of hymns for a chorus in four parts, in which parts for alternate single voices occasionally appear also. The composer who was first associated with Neri in his beneficial labors was Animucia, chapel-master to the pope, and afterwards Palestrina. These sacred plays, or "Azioni sacre," were divided into two parts. The sermon was delivered after the first part; but the performance interested the congregation so much "that there was no danger, during the sermon, that any of the hearers would retire before they had heard the second." As these "Azioni sacre" were not performed in the church itself, but in an adjoining hall or room called an "oratory," or, in Italian, *oratorio*, this title has since been applied to this species of sacred musical drama.

Though the oratorio gained wider form hand

in hand with the secular drama called opera, its ideal sacred meaning and expression rest upon the idea St. Philip Neri first introduced in his prayer-meetings. Like the first opera in Florence, the first oratorio was also composed and performed in Rome, in the year 1600. Its author is *Emilio del Cavaliere*, who played such a conspicuous part in the invention of the musical drama, and of whose labors I have treated in my lecture on the opera. "L'Anima è Corpo," written by a lady, Laura Guidiccioni, was the name of that first sacred musical drama, which was set to music by Emilio del Cavaliere. It was performed and acted on a stage erected, probably, in the oratory of the new church of Neri, the St. Maria, in Vallicella. It is curious to observe, that, in Rome, oratorios were represented and acted on a stage with decorations, like the opera, and principally at times of fasting, as late as the beginning of this century. I extract from Burney's "History of Music" the description of the first oratorio, "L'Anima è Corpo," or, rather, the directions which Emilio del Cavaliere gives for the performance and composition of a similar work:—

"It is recommended to place the instruments of accompaniment behind the scenes, which, in this first oratorio, were the following: A double lyre, a harpsichord, a large or double guitar, and two flutes.

"1. The words should be printed, with the verses correctly arranged, the scenes numbered, and characters of interlocutors specified.

"2. Instead of the overture, or symphony, to modern musical drama, a madrigal is recommended, as a full piece, with all the voice-parts doubled, and a great number of instruments.

"3. When the curtain rises, two youths, who recite the prologue, appear on the stage; and, when they have done, *Time*, one of the characters in the Morality, comes on, and has the note with which he is to begin given him by the instrumental performers behind the scenes.

"4. The *chorus* are to have a place allotted them on the stage, part sitting and part standing, in sight of the principal characters; and, when they sing, they are to rise and be in motion, with proper gestures.

"5. *Pleasure*, another imaginary character, with two companions, are to have instruments in their hands, on which they are to play while they sing and perform the ritornels.

"6. *Il Corpo*, the Body, when these words are uttered, '*Si che hormia alma mia*,' &c., may throw away some of his ornaments, as his gold collar, feather from his hat, &c.

"7. The *World*, and *Human Life* in particular, are to be gayly and richly dressed; and, when they are divested of their trappings, to appear very poor and wretched, and at length dead carcasses.

"8. The symphonies and ritornels may be played by a great number of instruments; and, if a violin should play the principal part, it would have a good effect.

"9. The performance may be finished with or without a dance. If without, the last chorus is to be doubled in all its parts, vocal and instrumental; but, if a dance is preferred, a verse beginning thus: '*Chiostri altissimi, e stellati,*' is to be sung, accompanied sedately and reverentially by the dance. These shall succeed other grave steps, and figures of the solemn kind. During the ritornels, the four principal dancers are to perform a ballet, "*saltato con capriole,*" enlivened with capers or *entrechats*, without singing, and thus, after each stanza, always varying the steps of the dance; and the four principal dancers may sometimes use the *galiard*, some times the *canary*, and sometimes the *courant* step, which will do very well in the ritornels.

"10. The stanzas of the ballet are to be sung and played by all the performers within and without."

These instructions will serve to give an idea of the oratorio in its infancy. It is also curious to observe the conspicuous part the ballet, or dancing, played in these early oratorios. Here is a chorus from "*L'Anima è Corpo.*"

12.

The development of the different forms of the sacred musical drama, such as the aria, the recitativo, the duet, and the chorus, was influenced by that of the opera. But though the melodious flowing aria, and expressive recitativo, replaced the old liturgical chants and psalmodies, composers strove to wed adequate music to sacred words; and thus, in the course of time, a distinct line of demarcation was drawn between the musical forms and contents of the oratorio and those of the opera.

Among the Italian composers who contributed most to the advancement of the musical drama, and especially of the oratorio, I must mention *Carissimi*, born about 1604, in Marino, near Rome. Carissimi, who devoted the greater part of his labors to the development of the sacred *cantata*, and who deserves so much credit for the perfection of the recitative, composed quite a number of oratorios, full of noble music. Some of the choruses are rich and grand in their effect. Among the oratorios which he composed are "Jephtha," "Solomon's Judgment," "Belshazzar," "Jonas," "The History of Job," "David and Jonathan," "Abraham and Isaac," &c. Italian composers of importance, who lived at this epoch, and who also composed oratorios, were Stradella, Scarlatti, Caldara, Colonna.

Though the form and the name of the oratorio are of Italian invention and origin, yet, as we shall see, German Protestant composers, Handel and Bach, were destined to bring it to that high point of perfection which to-day stamps this noble form of musical drama as the ideal, the goal, to reach which few composers have the strength of talent and the necessary knowledge. Here, however, we have first to consider another species of oratorio, and its historical development, — the Passion oratorio, which has grown side by side with the oratorio proper.

The custom of representing, during Passion-week, in an epic-dramatic form, the Passion of Christ, dates back to the earlier period of the middle ages, and this became foremost among the miracle plays.* A priest recited the part of Jesus, another that of the Evangelist, and a third the other parts; the people (*turbæ*), the disciples, the Jews, &c., were represented by the chorus. This is the traditional manner in which it is still performed in the Sixtine Chapel in Rome. The dramatic element remains to a considerable degree in the back-ground; and the music, which is only sung in the form of chants, appears in a very subordinate way. In the sixteenth century, some Protestant congregations introduced the custom of having the Passion performed in an entire musical form. The oldest known Passion-music, by a Protestant composer, is to be found in *Keuchenthal's* hymn-

* An interesting remnant of this custom still exists, even in our days. In Oberammergau, in the southern part of Bavaria, the peasants perform and represent a Passion play, according to the old traditions, at intervals of ten years. In Spain, also, Passion plays are still occasionally performed.

book, published 1573.* The soliloquy is in recitative form: there are short choruses besides for the *turbæ*, or people; a four-part chorus opens and finishes it. Similar in construction is the Passion-music in Seleneca's hymn-book, 1587. Of greater artistic importance are the works of *Henry Schuetz*, born 1585, died 1672. Schuetz was a pupil of the celebrated master, Giovanni Gabrieli of Venice. Initiated into all the secrets of musical composition, he returned to Germany, and finally settled in Dresden as chapel-master to the elector, George I. Schuetz was an upright, conscientious, and earnest artist. Like a saint, he devoted the best fruits of his talent to the Church. Faithful and unshaken, he fulfilled his duties even through the horrors of that great calamity, the Thirty Years' War. His sphere of action was of the greatest influence on the development of German musical art. He earnestly endeavored to transplant to his native country all those forms of musical composition which Italy then possessed in such high perfection; and, though a pupil of the Italians, he stamped his works with his own powerful German individuality. I have stated, in my lecture on the opera, that Schuetz set "Daphne" to music, — the first opera which appeared in Germany. Besides madrigals, psalms, and sacred

* Carl von Winterfeld: Der Evangelishe Kirchengesang.

songs, he also composed several Passion oratorios; and the effective manner in which he wrote his choruses already points to Handel. They are great and powerful creations. It is Handelian spirit that already speaks to us, though Handel was not yet born when Schuetz died. He forms the first link of that long chain of great masters, who, through their immortal works, won for Germany the supremacy in modern musical culture. Schuetz's works may be considered as the foundation of the form of modern German oratorio music; though he has not, in fact, written an oratorio in our sense.

The Passion music by the Prussian chapelmaster, *John Sebastiani*, composed and published in 1672 (the year of Henry Schuetz's death), shows a progress beyond his predecessors. We meet here, for the first time, Protestant choral melodies, set and harmonized for different parts in an artistic manner,—a peculiarity Sebastian Bach made such an effective use of in his Passion oratorios and his cantatas. The biblical narration is no more in the forms of psalmody or chanting, as we find it yet in Schuetz's Passions, but in recitative form, accompanied with two violins, or violas and bass. The *turbæ*, or people, appear as a four-part chorus; but as the Evangelist, sung by a tenor voice, also joins in an independent manner, these choruses thus consist, properly, of five parts. In the sacred songs, or chorales, only the highest part was sung; the other voices were executed by violas and a bass. At the last verse of the closing chorale, all the parts, instrumental and vocal, joined. Here we have the fundamental form upon which Bach built his Passion oratorios.

I must here mention the peculiar manner in which that celebrated opera composer, *Reinhard Keiser*, composed and brought out in Hamburg, 1704, a Passion oratorio, entitled "The Bleeding and Dying Jesus." Hunold Menantes wrote the verses. The Evangelist reciting the biblical narrative, as had been the custom, was left out, and also the chorale; but, instead of that, three cantatas, resembling scenes from dramatic opera,—"The Lamentation of Mary," the Tears of St. Peter," and a sighing, sentimental love-song, sung by the "Daughter of Zion,"—were substituted. The work made quite a sensation when it was first performed in Hamburg. But, at the same time, it seems the poet and the composer were sharply censured from the pulpit for their innovation. Though this form could not establish itself, it greatly influenced future efforts. In the subsequent poem by Brockes, treating of the same subject, we have an attempt to unite the old tradition with this new manner. Between the original biblical narrative, he wrote verses of pious content, relating to the situation; and, at convenient points, the Protestant sacred song, the chorale, finds a place. Keiser composed music to this new version; also, Mattheson, Handel, and Teleman. Bach has also taken some of the verses of Brockes's poem for different arias in his Passion, according to St. John.

Before I speak of the works of Bach and Handel, it will be necessary, for the understanding and appreciation of many a peculiar point in these works, to examine the musical culture of Protestant Germany since the Reformation.

The deeply-rooted love of accompanying, with appropriate songs, all their occupations in the house and the field, as well as their religious service, is a peculiarity which has been, in all times, a prominent trait in the character of the German people; and to this we owe many a beautiful melody. Though the Catholic Church sanctioned and admitted only the Latin language at its regular church service, long before the Reformation, sacred people's-songs, with German words, were sung, alternately, with the Latin psalms and hymns in the Catholic churches of Germany. Similar German songs were regularly intermixed with the dramatic recitations of the miracle and mystery plays. Besides sacred people's-songs, there was also an abundance of charming secular songs; and the best German composers set and arranged them in three, four, five, and more parts. It was well that the great reformer, *Luther*, had such a high idea of art, and of music in particular. "I am not of the opinion, that, through the gospel, all arts should be banished and driven away, as some zealots want to make us believe; but I wish to see all arts, principally music, in the service of *Him* who gave and created them." Thus said Luther himself. He was passionately fond of music. He calls it one of the greatest gifts of the Creator, and assigned it the first place next to divinity; "for, like this," he says, "it sets the soul at rest, and places it in a most happy mood," — "a clear proof," says he further, "that the demon who creates such sad sorrows and ceaseless torments retires as fast before music and its sounds as before divinity. There is no doubt that the seed of many virtues exists in the minds of those who love music; but those who are not moved by it, in my estimation, resemble sticks and stones." As a means of education, he attached great importance to the influence of music. "It is beneficial," he says, "to keep youth in continual practice in this art, for it renders people intellectual: therefore, it is necessary to introduce the practice of music in the schools; and a schoolmaster must know how to sing, otherwise I do not respect him." After the establishment of the first Protestant church, Luther's greatest endeavor was to adorn it with a fitting musical service. To this end, he associated with himself *John Walter*, and *Conrad Rupf*, or *Rumpf*, both musicians in the chapel of Frederic the Wise, elector of Saxony. Luther and his associates selected and arranged some of the finest Latin hymns and German songs, as used already in the Catholic Church. Luther was not as narrow, in this respect, as Calvin and some others of the Reformers. He well appreciated those "many good songs and hymns, both Latin and German." — "Therefore," said he to Walter, "it is not right in those, neither can I praise them for banishing all the Latin Christian hymns from the Church, who think they are not good Protestants if they sing, or listen to the singing of, a Latin hymn. On the other hand, it is not less wrong to sing only Latin hymns for the congregation." Luther had the great faculty of appreciating the wants and the genius of the German people; and, in this manner, the reforms which he introduced in the Church of Germany found a welcome echo in the hearts of his nation. It is known that Luther has written many a powerful hymn, full of Christian resignation, and confidence in the everlasting decrees of God: but only three of the many sacred melodies which were once attributed to him are considered as his throughout; among which is the celebrated "*Eine feste Burg is unser Gott.*" He also wrote his catechism in verse, and had it set to music in four parts. The first Protestant hymn, or choral-book, is by John Walter, and was published 1524, at Wittenberg. It originated under the eyes of Luther, and he wrote a preface to it. The songs (some of them with Latin words) were set by Walter, in four, five, and six parts. The principal melody, with a few exceptions, is still assigned to the tenor. The custom of giving the melody to the highest voice, the soprano, did not come into general use until the latter part of the sixteenth century; as, also, the practice of arranging the songs with plainer harmonies. This was probably done for the better convenience of the congregations, who were accustomed to sing, as they still do, the principal melody in unison. John Walter, though not a creative talent, or a contrapuntist of great learning and facility, will always occupy a meritorious place in the history of music, as the first faithful co-operator of Luther in the establishment of the German Protestant sacred musical service. Another composer, whose works Luther esteemed very highly, was *Ludwig Senfle*, born, according to some, at Zurich, to others, at Basle. He was a pupil of H. Isaac, and chapel-master to the ducal court of Munich. Senfle was a composer and a contrapuntist of great resources and learning; his works, distinguished by ingenious contrapuntal, though clear and distinct, combinations, by natural freshness and poetical conception, were much admired in his time. Although Senfle was a Catholic, and engaged at a Catholic court, Luther was in intimate relations with him, and very often the reformer asked the musician to send him, or set for him, new motets and hymns. In a letter, of the year 1530, Luther asked Senfle the favor to set in different parts, for him, the melody to the eighth verse of the fourth psalm, "I will both lay me down in peace, and sleep; for thou, Lord, only makest me dwell in safety." Senfle's compositions always refreshed, consoled, and strengthened him. "I believe truly," he writes, "that the end of my life is near. The world hates me, and I am also sick of the world. The good and faithful Shepherd may take my soul. I already sing to my own self the antiphony, but I wish to have it set in an efficient manner." There is no room to mention all those composers who adapted, arranged, and harmonized already known melodies for the Protestant Church, and some of whose melodies are still sung by German Protestant congregations. Among the foremost, however, I will name *Leo Hassler*, born 1564, at Nuremberg, a composer and contrapuntist of great knowledge, and of fine artistic taste and invention; *John Eccard*, 1553, whose German part-songs are so fresh, ingenious, and spirited, and who is also the author of a selection of very fine sacred songs; and *Michel Prætorius*, celebrated as composer and writer on musical subjects. Prætorius was a man of great experience and education. He travelled much, was in Italy, and exercised, through his writings, a great influence on the development of musical art in Germany. He also contributed much towards the revolution in music which began in Italy, and spread, in the seventeenth century, all over Europe.

I have already mentioned, in a previous lecture, that the Calvinists of Switzerland and the Huguenots of France adopted the Psalms, versified by Clement Marot and Theodore de Bèze, for their musical service. These melodies, as far as can be ascertained, were also adapted from popular people's-songs, and harmonized, in a simple form, by Claude Goudimel and Claudin le Jeune. The principal melody is still assigned to the tenor. Many of these charming and truly sacred melodies found their way to the Protestant Lutheran Church; and even English composers adapted them to the English Church service (The "Old Hundredth" is one of those psalm-melodies).

Thus we see that the first reformers and the heads of the Protestant churches endeavored to make their congregations take part in the singing of hymns and psalms. Though efficient choirs yet existed in the principal churches, able to perform the more artistic settings of the sacred songs, composers, in order to interest the congregation in the singing of the hymns, were gradually obliged to abandon the old custom of assigning to the tenor the principal melody, and to invent and harmonize melodies fit to be sung in union by the whole congregation. With the introduction of organs in the churches, and the engagement of efficient organists, capable of sustaining the singing of the congregation with appropriate, simple, yet characteristic and solemn harmonies, the musical part of the Protestant churches assumed that character which renders it sacred people's-song, in the fullest expression of the word. Though not so rich in its forms as the mass of the Catholic Church, the Protestant chorale, in its noble simplicity and grandeur, influenced the musical education of German composers not a little; and, of these composers, Bach and Handel were the greatest.

John Sebastian Bach was born at Eisenach,

March 21, 1685. He was a musician of the fifth generation of one of the most musical families ever produced by any country. At the age of ten he was left an orphan, and thus came under the care of his brother, who was an organist at Ohrdruff, and who also gave him his first instruction on the harpsichord, or clavier. After filling the place of organist and "concert-meister" in Annstadt, Muelhausen, Weimar, and Anhalt-Koethen, he was appointed cantor and musical director at the Thomas School, in Leipzig, a position which he held until his death, July 28, 1750. The last years of his life were saddened by a painful disease of the eyes, which, through an unsuccessful operation, resulted in total blindness.

Bach's whole social career may be summed up in a few words. There are no *virtuoso* triumphs to be related, which, while they would have been the means of great pecuniary gains to him, might have won for him the prestige of romantic intrigues, and success also; and yet he was the greatest organist and performer on the harpsichord, — perhaps the greatest organist that ever lived! We have none of those great performances of his works to describe, on account of which princes and nobles, astonished at his genius, rivalled each other in seeking to place him at the head of their chapels. He was too upright and modest, too true to his German individuality. Italians, or Italianized-German composers, then had the upper hand; and yet Bach had no equal — unless in Handel — in the arts of counterpoint, as well as in that requisite which stamps real genius, — original melodious invention! In 1733, in the dedication prefixed to that sublime work, the B-minor Mass, the equal of which is only to be found in Beethoven's Missa Solemnis, the cantor Bach besought the elector of Saxony to protect him from certain diminutions of salary, to which he was entitled as chapel-master of two churches in Leipzig. The salary was already small enough. In the same dedication, he modestly requested the honorary title of court-composer, in return for which he offered to write church and orchestral music as often as the elector should demand it. He did not obtain the empty title until three years later; but no further opportunity of composing for the Church or other musical institutions was offered to him by the court of Dresden. They wanted sentimental opera-music in the Church also: there was no place to be found there for Bach's solemn, pious, noble strains. I have neither time nor space to give due consideration to Bach's works, of which he created an astonishing quantity. I shall limit myself, in this lecture, to his Passion oratorios, and to some remarks on his cantatas and chorales.

Bach's artistic career culminates in the forms of Protestant church music; and, of these, the Protestant sacred song, *the chorale*, received his continual attention. No other composer studied, and turned to his artistic benefit, the harmonic and melodic resources of the chorale, like Bach. In this point, he resembles Palestrina, who held a similar beneficial relation to the Gregorian chant; and, from this point of view, the two great masters embodied in their works that spiritual life and expression which took root in the mystic creed of their relative churches. In his cantatas, in his motets, in his oratorios, in his works for the organ,—everywhere we meet in Bach's works the chorale, from its simplest form of a plain four-part harmonization, to the most artificial combinations which the deepest knowledge of counterpoint can lend to the master. Everywhere it is made the vehicle of profound ideal contents. In his great cantatas, however, this art reaches its culmination. In the cantatas, all that touches man's soul most deeply, every feeling, every emotion, from the cradle to the grave, is revealed in compositions inexhaustible in richness of harmony, truthfulness of melodious expression, and the greatest variety of forms. He penetrates the spiritual depth of holy writ, raises its sense by means of his incomparable art, transfigures it in tone until its whole meaning is revealed. Bach's church music is a perfect exposition of the text which forms its foundation. He seems to have found at once the best forms for all his creations; even where he employs the most ingenious ones, it is impossible to detect the slightest constraint. The power which he possessed, of instantaneously placing himself in the frame of mind required by the exigencies of the text he had to set to music, must have been astonishing: from this only we can explain to ourselves the phenomenal production of such a vast number of works of the highest order. Bach is said to have composed five Passion oratorios. But, up to this time, only two are known and published; the one according to St. John, and that according to St. Matthew. The latter is the more perfect of the two. The formal arrangement of the St. Matthew's Passion is based upon that of Bach's predecessors. There is the narrative of the Passion of Christ, according to St. Matthew, recited in a recitative form by a tenor. The speech of Jesus, the parts of St. Peter, of the Priest, and of Pontius Pilate, are assigned to a bass voice, and the Jews are represented by a chorus. A second group, the ideal Christian congregation, and the Daughter of Zion, accompany the action with moral observations. The Protestant congregation, forming the third group, inter mixes the different situations with the singing of suitable chorales. It is not possible to give an adequate description of this beautiful work: it must be studied and heard. All that Bach's genius could reach lies unfolded, in immortal master-strokes, in this wonderful sacred poem. The composer, with rare tact and appreciation, knew how to make use of all the best that the forms of his predecessors and his contemporaries presented, in order to serve his own noble purposes. Great genius, and an extensive knowledge of the deepest secrets of musical science, were made the means of glorifying, of revealing the most sacred, the most profound emotions which religion grants to mankind.

Besides the Passion oratorios, Bach also composed a Christmas oratorio.

*G. F. Handel** was born Feb. 23, 1685, in the same year as his great contemporary, J. S. Bach. In my lecture on the opera, I have given the outlines of his artistic career. Handel also composed two Passion oratorios for Hamburg. The first, which he wrote while yet a mere youth, shows only in some points the future great master; and the other, full of admirable choruses and arias (the chorale is also employed in it), was, until lately, little known. Handel commenced his career in Lon-

* See Chrysander's excellent Biography of Handel.

don, as an opera-composer; but his great influence on the musical culture of England is to be looked for in his oratorios. While yet manager and composer of Italian operas, he had already brought out (in 1720) "Esther," his first oratorio; and, some time after, "Deborah and Athalia." It was only when, through the opposition of the English aristocracy, he found himself, after years of manly struggle, nearly a ruined man, that he devoted his whole genius to the oratorio. In the year 1737, his career as opera manager came suddenly to an end: his iron constitution broke down; his mental faculties were temporarily disturbed, and an attack of paralysis endangered his life. After a short sojourn at Aix-la-Chapelle, where he took the baths, he returned to London, and in quick succession created in his latter years those great sacred dramas, in which his genius, ripened by immense perseverance and almost universal experience, embodied in immortal tone-pictures the everlasting truths of men's loftiest aspirations. I need only allude to "The Messiah," "Samson," "Israel in Egypt," "Solomon," "Saul," "Jephtha," "Judas Maccabæus," &c. As opera-composer and manager, Handel had already done the work of a very industrious man's life; besides a vast number of remarkable works, such as anthems, motets, psalms, hymns, cantatas, &c., which were composed during that time. It fills us with awe when we consider the quantity of gigantic works which he produced after he had passed his fifty-third year. Handel, through his failure as an opera-manager, was thus destined to give the oratorio its lasting form ; and his oratorios prove, that in this form he could realize, in the highest sense, those great ideas of dramatic life which were an inner necessity of his artistic mind. In the Holy Scriptures he found his immortal heroes, — the ideal type of Christian ambition and virtue: there also he found those words of consolation and hope which he so wonderfully wedded to the most exquisite and most tender strains ; there he also found those great principles of truth, religion, and liberty, which he triumphantly proclaimed to the world by means of his powerful, highly-spirited, and incomparable choruses. Not in the rigid forms of purely church music, neither in the empty superficial forms of the opera of his days, but in a noble universal human expression, lay the mission allotted to his exceptional genius to fulfil.

Though the English composers, Arne, Arnold, Stanley, Green, Worgan, and others, have also composed oratorios, their works had only a temporary success, and have since sunk into oblivion. The oratorie, in our sense, has never been earnestly and successfully cultivated in France: all the French composers of any note have almost exclusively devoted their best efforts to the opera. In Italy, the influence of the opera on church music was most enervating. The oratorios by such composers as Jomelli, Paisiello, Zingarelli, Cimarosa, Guglielmi, cannot be distinguished from their operas, except by a few choruses in the fugue form. In France and Italy, oratorios were generally performed in Lent only, when the performance of operas was suspended. The Italian and French composers, "treading without much thought on the path which the poets had broken up for them, proceeded to treat the oratorio like the opera-seria, though less restrained in their handling of this form, on account of its smaller dramatic requirements. We find no very essential difference between the two: arias, recitatives, choruses, are worked out in much the same way; only we observe the bass admissible as a solo voice first in oratorio. Neither poetry nor music possessed a really church-like character: composers modified their oratorio style merely in an outward manner. An oratorio air would have suited a similar situation in a serious opera: an operatic chorus might have been placed in an oratorio, &c. Both oratorio and opera were considered by songstresses and *castrati* as opportunities for the display of mechanical dexterity; though, indeed, a certain limit to it was drawn in oratorio. The direction which art took fully agreed with the wishes of the public: the latter expected to find as much enjoyment from oratorio (when this was fixed upon in celebration of any solemnities) as the opera could present." * In Germany, the forms of the Italian opera also exercised great influence on the oratorio and church music in general. The Italianized works of Teleman, Hasse, and Graun, instead of those of Handel and Bach, were the models of all German composers of any significance. With few exceptions, the oratorios of these musicians, composed of sentimental, long, and empty arias, and dry and spiritless contrapuntal choruses, were then of very little influence on real German musical art-culture. I must also mention the Passion oratorio, the "Death of Jesus," by the composer Graun. *C. H. Graun*, born 1701, and the favorite composer of Frederic the Great, was held up by his German contemporaries as the model composer; and his "Death of Jesus," performed in Berlin every Good Friday, was for a long time considered as the work *par excellence*, written in a flowing style. Graun, who then held the same position in Germany as that which Mendelssohn holds in public

* Otto Jahn: Mozart.

opinion to-day, is now as much underrated as he was once overrated. He has written some very effective and purely constructed choruses. Other German composers of this period, whose works still present some fine points, were Homilius, who has composed a Passion oratorio in a noble and pure style, Naumann, Krebs, Stölzel, Rolle, Schicht, and Ph. E. Bach, the son of J. S. Bach. The close imitation of the text of the Bible, and even the selection of the entire subject from Holy Writ, so piously adhered to by Handel, and in a great measure by Bach, in their grandest works, was entirely abandoned; and the words, in the form of operatic libretti, *Azioni sacre*, arranged and dramatized by Zeno and Metastasio, were the models for poets, and eagerly sought for by composers. "La Betulia Liberata," an oratorio libretto by Metastasio, was such a favorite text, that, from 1734 to 1828, Italian and German composers set it to music over and over again; even in 1771, Mozart tried his young powers on it. "Davide penitente," also by Mozart, is a transformation of a mass into an oratorio.

Bach's vocal works were laid aside in Germany; while, in England, Handel's oratorios took from year to year a deeper root in the hearts of the English people. The regeneration of the opera by Gluck, and the progress of instrumental music, gave, however, new and richer forms and contents to the art. It was in 1791, on a visit to London, that *Joseph Haydn*, born March 13, 1732, and the creator of the string quartet and the modern symphony, heard, probably for the first time, some of Handel's oratorios performed. Inspired by the sublimity of these works, he afterwards composed the "Creation" and the "Seasons." Haydn, always original, has also given us, in the oratorio form, music purely of his own. The music of his oratorios can be compared "to a charming garden, blooming among green meadows and refreshing, shadowy bushes; while Handel reminds one of imposing mountains, crowned with noble forests of cedars and oaks." The "Creation" and the "Seasons" are well known and admired; and they will remain so as long as men are capable of enjoying pure, spirited, and healthy music. Through Haydn, the instrumental accompaniment of the oratorio has been made the agency of greater and richer effects. *Beethoven's* "Mount of Olives," composed in 1800, is the only effort the great master made in the oratorio form. We also possess the fragment of an oratorio by the genial *Franz Schubert*, "Lazarus," which was performed for the first time in 1863. Though masters like *F. Schneider*, *L. Spohr*, *B. Klein*, *K. Loewe*, *The Chevalier Neu-*

kom, composed many a meritorious oratorio,— I need only mention Schneider's "Weltgericht," Spohr's "Letze Dinge," Klein's "David," — they were all surpassed by the popularity which *Mendelssohn's* oratorios gained in Germany as well as in England. Mendelssohn, endowed with a fine perception and a keen eye, under stood at once the depth and the power of Han del's and Bach's oratorios and other choral works. It was he who in 1829 had Bach's St. Matthew's Passion oratorio performed in Berlin under his own direction. The sublime work had then slept a sleep of one hundred years: for it was performed for the last time by Bach on Good Friday, 1729. How much Mendelssohn owes to his great models, every one acquainted with Bach's and Handel's works knows; but to what a great and effective use he turned his many resources, his two fine oratorios of "St. Paul" and "Elijah" have proven. Mendelssohn, more lyric than dramatic, more refined than profound, more conventional than original. who mastered the whole formal material of his art with such wonderful facility, ease, and *aplomb*, was thus understood and appreciated at once; and if we study the whole situation of musical art when "St. Paul" first appeared, we cannot help thanking the talent that produced it and through it gave new impulses to musical art.

His contemporary, *Robert Schumann*, the greatest composer since Beethoven's death, has also composed an oratorio, though of a secular character, "Paradise and the Peri." This beautiful work is, as Schumann's vocal works in general are, too seldom heard here. Schumann, original and profound, exquisite, ever femininely beautiful in his tender strains, and of imposing grandeur in his large forms, like all true original geniuses who adhere more to principle than to speculation, passed away before he found a deserved recognition.

These are the historical outlines of that noble art-form, the oratorio, with as much detail as my limits would allow me. It may be said that the oratorio is the highest form of musical dramatic art, in the sense that it possesses as foundation and contents the deepest and loftiest ideas of Christian religious-moral life. Its heroes and heroines are the ideal instruments and messengers of divinity. Their struggles, their triumphs, are those of high and noble souls. The strains with which the composer expresses their emotions, their feelings, must thus aim at the freest and most ideal perfection. Though the oratorio makes use of the same musical forms as the opera, yet, being uncontrolled by the inevitable action of the opera performer and the visible changes of stage machinery, it can develop these forms freely, and thus gain deeper musical meaning. The chorus, forming one of the most important factors in the oratorio, not seldom concentrates in itself all the rays of the central idea of the composer's sacred, dramatic expression and inspiration. The purely sentimental, the realistic passionate, — the reflex of human life in its continual conflicts and struggles, and the necessary basis of the opera, — do not find such a conspicuous place in the oratorio; and those composers who endeavor to transform the ideal form of the oratorio, by means of the dramatic element in the sense of the modern opera, will always see their own efforts, in spite of talent and knowledge, fall short of the most sanguine expectations. In my opinion, it is only through a return to a deep, earnest, and faithful study of the immortal works of those great oratorio composers, Handel and Bach, that a new foundation and a new contents can be regained. Were not Haydn and Mendelssohn inspired by these wonderful creations? And though they also created fine and classical works, yet they did not reach, far less did they surpass, their great models: therefore let us go back to that inexhaustible original mine of abundant treasures of beauty and inspiration, — not in the sense of mere superficial imitators and transcribers, but in that of the best spirit of our own times, — to strengthen, tc intensify, to enlarge our own minds through the ennobling influence of such everlasting and perfect models. No age has yet produced fine works independent of those productions that preceded it; and no age will fulfil its own artistic mission in its full significance, by wilfully ignoring the great, the beautiful creations which other ages before it have already accomplished.

FOURTH LECTURE.

The Opera, from its First Invention in Italy to the Death of Gluck.

UNTIL the close of that great epoch in musical history, marked by the immortal works of Palestrina, Orlandus Lassus, and their contemporaries, the composer's highest endeavor has been to adorn the Church with the noblest and purest products of his mind: for, as I have already stated, the whole mode of thought and life of the different European nations took root in the all-embracing idea of the Church; and art, especially music, emanated from the bosom of the Church. Though secular music was also diligently cultivated by different composers, to serve as a fitting adornment for social gatherings, its whole coloring yet bore the stamp of the domineering church music: even favorite people's-songs (folk-songs), as we have already seen, were worked up by the most distinguished composers in their masses, and as such became the property of the Church. Until the close of the sixteenth century, all forms which were admitted in musical practice consisted of those in many parts in simultaneous progression,—in two words, of choral music. Monody was not yet known; at all events, it was not yet in general use. In the form of chorus, the single individual, with his or her own characteristic feelings, disappeared among the multitude of people, who, moved by the same motives, by the same inward and outward causes, expressed their emotions, their feelings, in a collective manner: and, as in the middle ages, the rights of the individual in a psychological, social, and political sense were scarcely yet recognized, but entirely governed and controlled by the State and the Church, choral music, in its different forms, was the fitting expression of the artistic aspiration of these times. So we find the secular song in its divers aspects,—the chanson, the German lied, the glee, the villota, the villanella, and the charming madrigal, which represent almost exclusively the chamber-music of the fifteenth, sixteenth, and seventeenth centuries, always set for three, four, five, six, and more voices.

Monody, the expression of all those various lights and shades of individual inner life, was, then, yet excluded from practice in musical art. Its importance was not yet known or felt. Though the Church admitted chanting,—a stiff and monotonous monody,—the favorite form of composers was the chorus. With the acquirement of greater freedom in the political and social situation of the people, and with an increasing love for, and need of, the study of secular arts and sciences, these latter more and more adapted themselves in their forms to the character of the secular position they were to fill. But secular music, above all other arts, became, by means of this secular character, so prominent, that its influence, though at first beneficial in many respects, proved in the end to be deteriorating to the sacred meaning of church music.

Music, born at the altar of the Christian Church, borrowed at first all its forms from it. It already played a considerable part in those early, yet loosely dramatized plays, called moralities, or mysteries, rudely arranged by priests and monks from biblical or legendary subjects. They were performed in the middle ages, even in the churches, all over Europe: for mankind has a natural propensity for mimic representations of actual or feigned characters or deeds; and history tells us that all civilized, and even half-civilized, nations have had plays adapted to their individuality for religious festivities and amusements. The musical portion which formed a part of these mysteries and moralities consisted entirely of chorales and psalmodies or chants, taken from the church service. In my lecture on the oratorio, I have treated more fully of this peculiar custom. Though the opera also took root from these mystery or miracle plays, I only touch this ground here for mere comprehension's sake.

The practical event, however, which increased the love for the study of sciences, arts, and poetry, principally at the courts, and in many free cities, of Italy, was the conquest of Constantinople by the Turks under Soliman, in 1453. Though the Byzantine empire was utterly demoralized under the corrupt and weak government of Constantinople, the traditions of Greek and Roman greatness in art and science yet existed; and many a devoted scholar cultivated them. Through the conquest of Constantinople by the Turks, these scientific and literary men fled to other Christian countries, principally to Italy, and bequeathed to their new homes their learning and its refining consequences. Thus the study of old Greek literature increased rapidly: the past greatness of that wonderful nation awakened in the bosom of many an Italian student a desire to see his own nation produce the same wonders in art and poetry one day. The Greek drama, especially, was the subject of the closest study; and to restore it to its former magnificence was the dream of many a modern Greek scholar. After again deciphering the dramas of the old Greek poets, the men of letters could of course be no more satisfied with the crude, and in many respects coarse, representations of the miracle-plays. But to re-possess the Greek drama, in all its beauty and significance, it was soon found necessary to resuscitate the Greek music, as music always made an essential part of the drama of the old poets; and Greek writers were lavish in praise of the wonderful effects of that music. To discover this lost art again was, no doubt, the deep desire of many a modern Greek student and musician. It was at the same time felt that the monotonous chant, and the complicated contrapuntal choruses of the Flemish and Italian church composers, could not answer the wants of the Greek drama or of the drama in general. In order to understand the words of the poetry,—to follow their expression and meaning in all the different colorings of the drama,—a manner of singing was to be found, for which a more natural and logical rhythm, and a greater simplicity of harmony, were the necessary means. That the Greeks possessed this music was thought evident. But what were these forms of Greek music? How were those choruses arranged which played such an eminent part in the Greek drama? To solve these problems, nothing was left to consult on the real nature of Greek music but the exaggerated praises of the old authors.

Though all over Italy the different cities rivalled each other in the getting-up of scenic representations in which music formed a conspicuous part, it was principally in Florence, however, that, under the reign of the rich and art-loving house of the Medicis, music was destined to take a new direction, and to create for itself new and richer forms, sprung from this searching into the final supposed resuscitation of the lost Greek music. In Florence, more than anywhere else, the question of re-establishing the Greek drama vividly occupied the minds of literateurs, artists, and amateurs: it was the theme of daily discussions at court and in literary circles. The house of *Giovanni Bardi*, Count of Vernio, a man of great accomplishments, and poet and composer himself besides, was, among others, the place of meeting of those enthusiastic Hellenes who were not satisfied with theoretical discussions on the possibility of the re-establishment of the Greek drama alone, but, being men of deeds, who began to put their admitted theories in practice. The principal men who frequented Bardi's house (and afterwards, when, in 1592, Pope Clemens VIII. called Bardi to become his *maestro da camera*, that of Corsi) were *Vincenzo Galilei*, *Pietro Strozzi*, *Girolamo Mei*, *Ottavio Rinuccini*, *Giulio Caccini*, and some time after, also *Jacopo Peri*. These men unanimously proclaimed the means of the musical forms then in use, as insufficient to answer the requirements of a truly musical drama; and Vincenzo Galilei, the father of the great mathematician and astronomer, Galileo Galilei, was foremost among them as champion for Greek music. Galilei was a pupil of the distinguished composer and theorist, Zarlino: he was also an able performer on the lute. Galilei wrote and published, in opposition to Zarlino, a pamphlet in the form of a dialogue, in which Bardi and Strozzi appeared and discussed the merits of ancient and modern music; and of which the conclusion is, that modern music is only fit for the uncultivated masses, and therefore to be despised by the connoisseur. Galilei was not yet satisfied with giving his ideas on the nature of true music to the world; but he also composed, for one voice, the scene of Count Ugolino in Dante's "Inferno," and performed it himself with an accompaniment on the viola. Being much applauded in this first effort, he afterwards set some of "Jeremiah's Lamentations" in a similar way to music. This form of song, which Galilei designated *monody*, seems to have been really the first of composition for one voice independent of counterpoint.

The singer Giulio Caccini, called the Roman, was one of the most zealous disciples of the new theories, and also a frequenter of the meetings at Bardi's and Strozzi's. He set, in imitation of Galilei, different poems to music for one voice, which he afterwards published in 1601, under the title of "Nuove Musiche." Caccini gave to his work a long preface, in which he put forward his claims to the accomplishment of the new manner of musical composition. He also gave instructions concerning a good method of singing; and, to judge from his musical illustrations, the art of singing must have been already advanced to a high degree of perfection. Another master, *Ludovico Viadana*, has also great claims to be considered as one of the first composers of pieces for one voice. In 1602, he published a number of "Concerti da Chiesa" for one, two, three, and four voices, with an accompaniment for the organ. In the preface, he says that he composed these Concerti as early as 1595; and, encouraged by his friends, he published them to serve in place of the motets, originally written for five, six, and more parts, and of which one part was sung by a single voice, while the organist played the other parts. As the forms of instrumental music were at this period yet in a state of infancy, choral music, and, in particular, madrigals, were roughly adapted to the wants of the instrumental resources then in use. Viadana, with a more refined sense, perceived the defects of such an inartistic custom, and thus tried to substitute a better and a more musical manner through his concerti. These pieces are in melodious quality far superior to the monodies of Galilei and Caccini: they can be considered, indeed, as the first musical productions in cantilene style, written in a smooth, singable, and very melodious manner.

The greatest and most important step towards the establishment of musical drama was now made. The next thing to be done was to make use of the new means, in a dramatic work, destined to consist of adequate music from beginning to end. Several of the musicians who were accustomed to be present at the literary meetings mentioned before, excited by the novelty of the subject, had already tried to realize the idea of having the whole drama set to music, and sung.

The first whom history mentions, as having tried his hand at the new form of drama, was Emilio del Cavaliere. Two pastorals, "Il Satiro" and "La Disperazione di Fileno," by the renowned poetess Laura Guidiccioni, were given in 1590, at the court of Florence; and another,

"Il Giuco Della Cieca," followed in 1595: all three were set to music by Emilio del Cavaliere, and sung throughout.

According to Arteaga ("History of the Opera in Italy"), the musical part was written in the style of the madrigal, and was full of tedious artificialities and repetitions. It seems, however, that E. del Cavaliere's efforts in the new direction did not satisfy the modern Hellenes who assembled at Bardi's.

It was reserved to another to fulfil, in a high degree, the so long-delayed expectations of the impatient members of the literary circle. I have already stated, that, after Bardi's engagements in Rome, the meetings of the club, or academy, were held at the house of Jacopo Corsi, who, like Bardi, entertained the same views of the necessity of discovering a new musical form, to be adopted for the so-called Greek dramatic purposes. It is in Corsi's house that we meet *J. Peri* for the first time. Peri was a good musician; and, through a happy stroke, he brought the new and so diligently sought for musical-dramatic form into existence. The poet Rinuccini, who had already written the intermezzo "Combattimento d'Appollino col Serpente," and which was put on the stage with choruses composed by the celebrated madrigal composer, Luca Marenzio, re-wrote and re-arranged this intermezzo called it "Daphne," and intrusted it to Peri, who set it entirely to music, and had it performed at Corsi's house. The work received general applause. Peri made use for the first time here of the *stilo rappresentativo*, *recitativo*, *or parlante*, — a kind of musical form which holds the medium between well-formed melody and speech. It was the beginning of a recitative style: every one present was delighted; and no one doubted but that the music which the old Greeks had used in their dramas was thus recovered. In the year 1600, on the occasion of the marriage of Mary de Medicis with Henry IV., King of France, among other festivities, a new work by Rinuccini also was produced at Florence, called "Euridice, una Tragedica per Musica." It was greeted by the brilliant assembly of nobles and artists with still greater applause than "Daphne." Peri allowed Caccini, who had also composed music to Rinuccini's "Euridice," to have some of it performed at the first representation; but he afterwards published his own setting of the poem.

In "Euridice," we now possess for the first time all the forms of our opera, though still in a merely primitive state. At the time when Peri's "Euridice" appeared in Florence, E. del Cavaliere had performed his allegoric drama in Rome, "L'anima è Corpo," of which I have spoken in my lecture on the oratorio. These early musical dramas were composed of simple choruses in the madrigal style, and of musical recitation: in some lyric moments, the arioso style already appeared at times; but as these first opera-composers attempted, as they fancied, to imitate the musical forms which they believed the Greeks had used in their dramas, the musical part of their works never attempted a broad, well-formed melody. It was purely musical declamation. The instrumentalists who played the accompaniments in "Euridice" were placed behind the scenes. The only instrumental piece, somewhat resembling an air, and which introduces a scene in the first opera, consists of fourteen bars: it is called a "Zinfonia," and was to be played by three flutes (see the lecture on instrumental music). But all the material for formation and construction of the opera was thus discovered; and, in the course of time, an art-work emerged from these precocious efforts which was destined to play a conspicuous *rôle* in the artistic and social life even of whole nations. I will here give as specimens (for the sake of comparison), a recitative and chorus from "Euridice," as composed by Peri and Caccini to the same words.

13. *RECITATIVO.* *Peri.*

14. *RECITATIVO.* *Caccini.*

15. *CHORUS of the Infernal Gods.* ***Peri.***

16. *CHORUS of the Infernal Gods.* *Caccini.*

Though the newly-discovered style, the *stilo recitativo*, created such a sensation all over

Italy, the better composers looked upon it as a mere production of amateurs not very much skilled in musical science; and of course they had no inclination to cultivate the new form. But progress in the new direction was not to be retarded; for, soon after, a master of great musical talent and ability directed his attention to the "drama per musica," or the opera, as it was afterwards called: and this master was *Claudio Monteverde*, born 1568, in Cremona. Monteverde was at first, for some time, chapel-master at Mantua; and, from 1613 until his death in 1643, he occupied the same position at St. Marc's Cathedral in Venice. Though the works which he composed for the Church already bear the marks of decadence in style, when compared with the classic works of Palestrina and his school, they yet give evidence of great strength and invention in the master. But, with his madrigals and operas, he marks the beginning of a new era in musical art. Monteverde was no longer satisfied to write merely fine and scientific contrapuntal works: his aim was to render impressively the different sentiments of the poem he endeavored to wed to music. Though he exposed himself to the severest criticisms of the purists of his time, he would not shrink back from the use of the sharpest dissonances to serve his artistic purposes, always directed to the dramatic expression of his nature. That such a man was needed to give a solid form to the opera, a foundation which would secure it permanence, and draw into his service talented composers, is evident; and, at the same time, his efforts proved beneficial to the new art-form and modern musical art in general. Monteverde's first opera was Rinuccini's "Orfeo," and afterwards "Arianna" and "Il Ballo delle Ingrate," from the same poet's pen. "Arianna" seemed to have pleased the most, especially the lament of the deserted Arianna; for all Monteverde's contemporaries speak of it with the greatest admiration. The dramatic works of this composer show a great progress beyond those of his predecessors. Everywhere we see the tendency to give to the words and to the characters of his poem the necessary true musical expression gained by an effective use of harmonic means and analogous rhythm. As Peri himself said, in his preface to the printed copy of his "Euridice," the new manner of composing required a new form of harmonic accompaniment, — an accompaniment, which, while at the same time it sustained the singer, would not interfere with his freedom of dramatic action. Monteverde went still further, and used his instrumental means for the suitable characteristic coloring of different dramatic situations; and we already find in his operas quite a number of instrumental pieces, such as symphonies, ritornellos, toccatas, romanescas, and ricercares, introducing and closing the scenes.

The opera soon became the favorite entertainment of the different courts of Italy, which also soon vied with each other in the most brilliant, dazzling, fantastic, and extravagant representations and stage effects; and, as we shall see hereafter, singers with extraordinary vocal powers, and the show of brilliant costumes and machineries, drove the idea of the real meaning of dramatic musical art in Italy entirely into the background.

Italian church composers, seeing the brilliant career of the opera, took hold of it with all their energy; and thus the progress the new art-form made was rapid. As there is no room here to mention all the men who appeared as opera composers, I shall restrict myself to the principal ones, as in their works we perceive the different phases and changes which operatic forms went through in the course of time. Foremost among those masters were *Francis Colleto*, called *Cavalli*, *Giacomo Carissimi*, and *Marco Antonio Cesti*. The recitative of these masters is, in some of its parts, written with great dramatic truth and variety. It already shows, as it ought to do, an entirely different treatment from that of the air, with which it forms those necessary points of dramatic contrast and gradation. Though Carissimi, as far as we know, did not compose any operas, but devoted his energy and knowledge to the forms of the oratorio and the chamber cantata, which replaced the madrigal, his airs and recitatives are full of vigorous dramatic life and spirit. Here is a recitative from his oratorio "Jephtha." What an immense progress beyond Peri and Caccini!

17.

A pupil of Carissimi's, *Allessandro Scarlatti*, born in 1659, bore a still greater share in the progress of modern musical forms after the discovery of the opera. To Scarlatti belongs the merit of having founded the Neapolitan school of music, out of which came forth a large array of distinguished composers and singers, whose influence in musical matters was felt till up to our modern times. Scarlatti has written remarkable works in every form of musical composition in practice in his time; and an astonishing number of these. He perfected the recitative, and gave it classic value. His arias, though wanting in breadth and largeness, are models of fresh, melodious, refined musical forms. His orchestral accompaniments are graceful, never overladen, but always effective, considering the time in which he lived.

The Italian opera was soon transplanted to all the different courts of Europe, where it remained as the exclusive spectacle of princes and nobles. The prestige of Italian opera composers was so great, that in Germany, in England, a composer could only succeed when he gave himself entirely up to the Italian style of writing. France, however, though admitting the fundamental idea of the Italian opera, created a work in many respects materially different; and, as we shall see, this bore in itself the germ of the modern musical drama. Cardinal Mazarin transplanted the opera into France, and *R. Cambert* was the first French composer who composed an opera (about 1660). Cambert's operas are nothing but crude efforts, reminding one more of church psalmody than of secular music for the stage; but his successor, *Jean Baptist Lully*, born in the year 1633, though an Italian by birth, identified himself so closely with the French spirit and natural characteristics, that the existence of entirely French opera is due to him. He had the talent to gain the favor of Louis XIV.; and, with that, all the advantages necessary to put his idea about the musical drama in realization. Lully's greatest merit was that of having invented the form of the overture. Instead of the short introduction generally employed by Italian composers, his overtures are an elaborate form in two parts; the first of which was usually broad and of a slow movement; the second of a spirited cast, habitually a fugue: sometimes a minuetto, or another piece in a favorite dance form, closed the whole. Lully's overtures were much admired by his contemporaries, and imitated in formal construction. Another specialty which distinguished Lully's opera from the Italian, was the introduction of the dance, or the ballet, which the French opera has retained as an important feature until our days. A third, and a not less significant specialty of the French opera was the greater importance the chorus was allowed to take: through this, it gained more dramatic life. That which imparted to the Italian opera its greatest charm — the recitative and the air — is yet an indistinct chaos in Lully's operas. Only here and there the simple song-form succeeded. The French, always anxious for a clear and distinct declamation of the words, were yet insensible to a free, broad, and well-defined melody (cantilena). Lully's next successors, such as Colasse, Charpentier, Campra, cultivated the French opera in the spirit of its creator; and it was reserved to *Jean Philippe Rameau*, born at Dijon in 1683, to give it a new impulse. Rameau, who was a fine performer on the organ and the harpsichord, and a distinguished theorist, was already fifty years old when he attempted to write his first opera "Hippolite and Aricie;" and he at once showed his great superiority over his predecessors. His melodic movements concentrate to logical forms full of character; his choruses evince the highest dramatic effect: but, above all, the part his orchestra has to play is as original as it is at times grand. In those scenes where a storm, a battle, a horrible earthquake, have to be depicted Rameau, in spite of the indifferent state of orchestral playing in his time, produces powerful and very characteristic effects. Lully's and Rameau's works, until the appearance of the chevalier Gluck, were esteemed above any other operas by the French people. The attempt to introduce the Italian opera in France failed signally for a long time; though the French singers who appeared at the Academie Royale de Musique could not compare (with their exaggerated and nasal singing) to the Italian *virtuosi* who first sung in Paris.

The history of the opera in England is nothing but a narrative of feuds and cabals between singers, foreign composers, and managers. The English musicians exercised little influence upon the growth of the musical drama. ***Henry Purcell***, born in 1658, who has shown, in the music he composed to plays, and in his operas, so much dramatic power, so much melodious freshness, died too young — at the age of thirty-seven — to take an active part in the formation of an original English opera-form; and it seems, besides, that he had not the necessary opportunity offered him of bearing with his whole genius and musical accomplishments on the advantageous growth of this important field. It is much to be regretted, for the sake of English musical culture, that such a profound talent should have passed away without finding a worthy successor among his countrymen. The composers who wrote for the English stage were Italians, and the great Handel. French influence, led by Cambert, whom his clever rival, Lully, had superseded at the court of Louis XIV., was, however, of not long duration. The picture which the musical life of London presents at this period is full of instruction and interest. The wealth of the English aristocracy commanded the greatest singers and composers; and, to judge from all the reports we possess of the operatic representations of this time, they must have thrown into shadow even what musical Italy could offer, with its hundreds of fine singers and composers. But did this preference for foreign musicians retard, discourage, and in many ways wrong the indigenous cultivation of English musical art, and above all that of the musical drama, — the opera? This has been often asserted, and, I truly believe, with something of injustice. The artistic genius of a nation will work its way out, in spite of religious, political, and social obstacles. Those men, who, through their strong individuality, through their powerful minds, mark an epoch in the life of nations, either in art or science, are nothing but the logical result of the aspirations of those nations.

England, as I have shown in a previous lecture, had an epoch in musical history — principally at that great Elizabethan age — rich in original and learned composers, many of whose vocal compositions, sacred as well as secular, are yet the delight of the connoisseur. Was the musical genius of the English nation exhausted after the death of Henry Purcell? Or was it wanting in those requisites so indispensable to the opera composer, — power and intensity of musical dramatic life, sensibility in passionate expression, &c? If fine representations and brilliant performances of great works exalt and stimulate to production the artist endowed with knowledge and genius, while at the same time he is able to form his taste and to exercise his judgment by such means, then the musicians of no other nation enjoyed such inestimable advantages in a higher degree than the English, principally during the whole of the eighteenth century. I cannot admit that their efforts, if equal or superior to those of the foreign composers, — their contemporaries, — would have been rejected or ignored by their nation or by foreign judges.

The greatest of all composers who have composed for the English stage was *G. F. Handel*, born at Halle, in Germany, in 1685. He received his first musical education from the organist Zachau, at his native city: he afterwards went to Hamburg, where the renowned Keiser produced his works. There he composed some operas, which were already noticed favorably. From Hamburg, where by teaching music he saved money enough to undertake a voyage to Italy, he went directly to this holy land of all young musical aspirants to fame. With energy and open eyes, he made himself master of all that Italy could offer him, as important and indispensable to a thorough composer. In Italy, he came in friendly intercourse with the greatest artists, such as Allessandro Scarlatti, his son Dominico Scarlatti, Corelli, &c. After an absence of three years, Handel came back to Germany; and, having made a reputation during his travels, the elector of Hanover offered him the position of chapel-master. On the invitation of some English nobleman, he visited England for the first time in 1710. On this first visit, he composed his opera "Rinaldo" for London; but it was not till the year 1712 that he took up his permanent home in the English capital, where he produced, in quick succession, work after work: and, as though his labors as a composer did not suffice to his energy, he also became an opera manager, — an undertaking which finally proved in many ways fatal both to his purse and to his health. Handel died April 13, 1759. The closing years of his life were saddened by blindness, at first partial, and finally complete.

I have only to speak of Handel's merits as an opera composer here. Though, through his great genius and his rich inventiveness, he created many an immortal aria and chorus, and though the dramatic truth and the power of his classic recitatives are unsurpassed by any other composer, yet he was not destined to realize in its whole signification, the ideal of a dramatic musical work for the stage, in which poetry and music concur to create dramatic characters, though fictitious, yet full of human reality,— characters that live with apparent truth in our imagination, heightened by the breath of musical inspiration, and almost forming a part of our own existence. This he was to realize, and in the most ideal sense, in that great art-form, which became the culminating point of his rich and laborious career,—the oratorio. Handel was conservative with regard to the Italian opera: he improved upon the forms of his predecessors, by enriching them with the gifts of his exquisite musical imagination; but he never stopped in his course to introduce reforms in the construction of the libretto submitted to him for musical composition. It was the defect of the Italian opera which he inherited; and, in spite of the many pearls with which he endowed this shadow of dramatic life, he could not save it from final death. Handel's operas, with the exception of some of the finest airs and choruses, have sunk into oblivion; and, in spite of the great musical beauties they contain, the rich source of pure enjoyment and instruction they present to the musical student, to revive them on the stage would prove a decided failure. Handel's importance for our modern times is to be looked for in his oratorios, and not in his operas

Soon after the invention of the opera in Italy, it found its way to Germany. Rinuccini's "Daphne," translated into German by Opitz, and set to music by Henry Schütz, was played, in 1627, before the court of the elector of Saxony at Torgau; but, the music being lost, it is not possible to judge of its form or of its merits. There is no time to name all the opera composers, and the works which they composed, for the many large or small courts of German princes. With the exception of the operatic performances at Hamburg, the whole state of dramatic musical life in Germany, until Gluck, is that of the reign of Italian singers, Italian composers, or, like Hasse, Graun, Naumann, Italianized German composers; though their works certainly possess many meritorious qualities. At Hamburg, a free and commercial city, full of enterprise and artistic aspirations, the opera, with the characteristics of German life, seemed for some time to succeed. A man, gifted with a fine talent for melody and uncommon facility of production, composed opera after opera for the Hamburg stage, — I mean *Reinhard Keiser*, born in 1673. Keiser's operas were played on the principal stages of Germany; and one of them was even brought out in Paris, which then meant a good deal. I have already stated, that Handel, in his youth, wrote a few operas for

Hamburg; but the efforts of the Hamburgians to establish a permanent opera, with German artists and composers at its head, were of no avail: the time was not yet ripe for the German mind to step in, and give the opera that form and meaning which it was susceptible of receiving in future years. The master who first understood the necessity of reforming the formal construction and the ideal meaning of the then existing Italian opera was a German, the Ritter *Gluck.*

As we have seen, the opera is entirely an invention of the Italians. Italian composers brought it to that point of comparative perfection in which other nations received and admired it; and only after making it thus a property of their own, were the French and the German composers enabled to mould its forms to the spirit and wants of their own national individualities. The Italian composer's first ambition is to write beautiful melodies. He proceeds with a certain artistic *naïveté* to the production of his works; but being, to a certain degree, a born artist, his artistic nature carries him safely over the breakers. He succeeds where the German and the French would signally fail, as these latter first stop to examine into the propriety, the possibility, of the thing; and, as long as the Italian opera composers had their own way, their reign was supreme all over Europe. Another advantage, which also aided them much, was the gift of beautiful voices, which the Italians possessed, and still possess, in so high a degree. From the earliest times, the Italian churches availed themselves of the fine voices found among their people; and thus, through years of diligent practice, a singing method established itself, which made the beautiful material still more beautiful and effective. With the invention of the opera, and its general introduction on all the stages of Italy, the art of singing received a new impulse. It is with amazement that we read of the energy, the perseverance, the almost passionate application, with which the Italians cultivated the art of singing then; and, as it proved a great source of pecuniary earnings, in order to satisfy an excessive ambition, and for money's sake, they shrank not back from any trials in order to obtain their end. In its first stadium, the opera offered gorgeous costumes, ingenious and brilliant decorations, dazzling scenes of allegoric and fantastic monstrosities, to the eye. The libretti, loosely cut after the pattern of Greek mythological plays, were written and arranged for the purpose of flattering, in exaggerated terms and pictures, the patrons of singers, composers, and poets, the vain princes and nobles, in whose presence, and for whose entertainment, the representations took place. The great passions — love, hatred, vengeance, heroism — were trifled with; and these ridiculous shepherds and shepherdesses, the braggadocios of these pampered heroes, the innocent thunders of these impossible gods and goddesses, can only now excite us to a smile. In the course of time, a somewhat better taste prevailed; and, instead of a mere feast for the eye, the ear became supreme. Through the efforts of Scarlatti and his pupils, and through the masters of the Venetian school, the forms of the recitative and the aria were fixed. Chorus, if it did not disappear entirely, was considered of minor importance. Yet, in spite of the talent and influence of such composers as Caldara, Colonna, Durante, Buononcini, Gasparini, Porpora, Traetta, Jomelli, the opera fell into another extreme: the exaggerated admiration of purely musically-fine execution, and the mere physical beauty of the voices, made the opera a medley of arias, only fit for the concert-room. The composer was the servant of the all-powerful *virtuosi*. The libretto, without regard, or with but little regard, to dramatic truth, had to be arranged so as to give to the best singers an opportunity to appear most often, and to display to great advantage the fine qualities of their voices and their wonderful execution. Besides, it was necessary to have the two best singers perform duets; and, if there was a third, also trios. (The bass voice, with very little exception, was excluded from solo parts, as unfit for *virtuoso* display.) It was therefore the business of the poet and the composer to procure these articles. The cut of the arias was always the same: the composer furnished the canvas, upon which the virtuoso, according to his or her fancies and abilities, and without regard to the sentiment which the dramatic situation required, embroidered those endless variations of passages, trills, skips, and long-sustained notes. That divine right which the modern composer claims, of having his melodies sung in the form and version in which he has written them down, did not then exist. On the contrary, that composer who best accommodated his talent to the caprices of the singers was the most popular; and his operas were performed in preference. "Therefore," says an old writer on music, "do we perceive an everlasting sameness in the operas of to-day. Any one who has heard or seen the representation of two operas has heard or seen the scenas of a hundred others." While the books of that time, by professional and amateur writers on music, are full of the feats, the extravagant behavior, and the large salaries, of singers, they tell us little of composers; and that little is not always to be trusted. Under these circumstances, we cannot help wondering if a composer yet succeeded in calling attention to his work, and in creating such pearls of musical form as we here and there discover in scarce old scores, now buried under the dust of libraries.

To the Italians belongs, to a great extent, the merit of having perfected the beautiful in a purely melodious direction; but the forms of their recitatives, their arias, their duets, and trios, once established and recognized, they became conventional. Thus the originality of the composer was fettered: his art sank to a mere business; and with it gradually sank the supremacy of the Italian opera. The Italians, so rich in beautiful melodies, from the graceful, naïve, and simple canzonetta, to the broad and heroic grand aria, were only destined to bring this side of the musical drama to its perfection. But the opera, as the highest expression of that art-form, — the musical drama, — in which poetry, architecture, painting, and the terpsichorean art, enlivened by the deepest and truest heart-beat of musical feeling, concur to present to the man of artistic sensibilities a richly heightened picture of human existence in all its different shades and lights, — a mirror of the ideal fancies of man's soul, — is not the work of one nation. The Italian art has only exclusive importance and signification for the Italian, the French for the

Frenchman, the German for the German, &c.; but the quintessence of that great spirit which governs and inspires them all in their art-productions, is the goal towards which the genius of mankind strives. One nation supersedes another, every one learning from the other; where one stops, another takes up the thread: every one is called to bring a certain part of the universal work of progress to its perfection. The imagination sees the goal; but will the human mind ever reach it?

Before I speak of the great reforms which Gluck introduced in the musical drama, let me insert a passage here by a musician, contemporary with Gluck: but the article from which I extract this passage was written before Gluck had brought out in Paris his "Iphigenia in Aulis;" and Gluck's greatest reputation and influence as a reformer only commenced with his success as an opera composer for the Paris stage. At the same time, it shows the current of thought with artists and people of good taste, judgment, and aim, at this remarkable period. "In that extraordinary spectacle," our author says, "to which the Italians have given the name of opera, there is to be found such a mingling of the great and the small, the beautiful and tasteless, that I hesitate in what terms to write about it. In the best of operas, we see and hear such stupid and trivial things, that we might think them only calculated for children, or for a childish populace; and, in the midst of this revolting silliness, passages occur that pierce the heart with horror, fear, pity, or refined voluptuousness. A scene during which we have forgotten ourselves, and felt the liveliest interest for the characters, is followed by one in which the same characters strike us as blundering fools, awkwardly trying to astonish and alarm a vulgar crowd. While we cannot bear to recall the senselessness that has disgusted us in the opera, we cannot help remembering its charming scenes with emotion, or without wishing that artists would unite to make of this great spectacle that perfect thing which it is capable of becoming. The opera might be the most powerful of all spectacles, because all the fine arts unite in it; but it is a proof of the superficiality of the moderns, that, in the opera, they have lowered, and exposed to contempt, all these arts." *

The artist, so much wished for, had already put into execution those means required for the regeneration of the musical drama; and that artist was Gluck.

Christoph Willibald Gluck † was born on the 2d of July, in 1714, at Weidenwang, in Bohemia.

* Sulzer: Theorie der schoenen Kuensten.

† Anton Schmid: C W. Ritter von Gluck, dessen Leben, &c.

After having received instruction in music in different places, and his parents not having the necessary means to provide for his further education, he went to Prague, and afterwards to Vienna, where he taught music, and sang or played in different church choirs and orchestras to make a living; while he studied, with what opportunities chance could offer him, the works of recognized masters, such as Caldara, Fux, Conti, Porsile. Through the kindness and generosity of a nobleman who took the young artist with him to Milan, he was enabled to receive lessons in the higher branches of composition from Samartini. Having finished his studies with Samartini, who initiated him in the arts and secrets of Italian-opera writing, he composed, with more or less success, different operas, according to the customary traditional forms, for divers Italian stages. After a short visit to Paris and London, where he was engaged to produce some of his operas, he returned to Vienna, which city he made his permanent home, and from whence he afterwards proclaimed those great ideas of a true musical drama which effected a revolution in the form of opera.

Gluck's plan of reform, and the necessary ability and intellectual understanding to carry out this plan, must have matured slowly; for, until the production and representation of "Orfeo," in 1762, he had written, like every other composer of his time, Italian operas. But the peculiar style and the dramatic spirit which distinguished the composer Gluck in the latter part of his life must, at times, have already appeared in his Italian operas; for the refined and courteous poet Metastasio wrote, in 1751,* "Gluck has surprising fire; but he is mad. He composed an opera for Venice which was very unfortunate. He composed others, with various success. I am not a man to pretend to judge him." In a letter, written in 1756, to the singer Farinelli, the poet says, *àpropos* of the operatic representations for some public festivity, "The drama is my 'Re Pastore,' set by Gluck, a Bohemian composer, whose spirit, noise, and extravagance have supplied the place of merit in many theatres of Europe, among those whom I pity, and who do not form the minority of the folks of the world." No doubt, while Gluck thus produced opera after opera in the Italian style, he became gradually aware of the unnaturalness and defects of the old form, as he at the same time noticed what what was good and essential for its future regeneration. Burney, who, on a visit to Vienna, had a conversation with Gluck on this subject, relates, that while in London, where Gluck pro-

* Burney: Musical Tour through Germany. &c.

duced his operà, "La Caduta de Giganti," he studied the English taste; remarked particularly what the audience seemed most to feel; and, finding that plainness and simplicity had the greatest effect upon them, he has, ever since that time, endeavored to write for the voice more in the natural tones of the human affections and passions, than to flatter the lovers of deep science or difficult execution. In London, Gluck was surely also struck by the beauties of Handel's works; but, to carry out his plan in its full strength, Gluck needed a poet penetrated with the same conviction of a necessary reform as he was, and who would understand and enter into his ideas. This poet he found in the person of *Calzabigi.* The first opera of this new and remarkable period of Gluck's artistic career was "Orfeo," performed at Vienna, the 5th of October, 1762. The dilettanti and the connoisseurs were not a little surprised at the boldness of the composer, and, at the first representation, opinions were divided about the merits of the new style. In 1766, "Alceste" appeared, the libretto of which was also by Calzabigi. In this new work, Gluck had broken entirely with the Italian opera. In "Alceste," which he composed in his fifty-third year, the full breadth and significance of his gradually-ripened ideas lay unfolded. In the preface, written in Italian,

Gluck himself sets those ideas forward.* "When I undertook to set to music the opera of 'Alceste,' I proposed to myself to avoid the abuses which the mistaken vanity of singers and the excessive complaisance of composers had introduced, and which, from the most splendid and beautiful of all public exhibitions, had reduced the opera to the most tiresome and ridiculous of spectacles. I wished to confine music to its true province, — that of seconding poetry by strengthening the expression of the sentiments and the interest of the situation, without interrupting the action, and weakening it by superfluous ornament. I thought that music ought to give that aid to poetry which the liveliness of coloring and the happy combination of light and shade afford to a correct and well-designed picture, — animating the figures, without injuring their contour. I have, therefore, carefully avoided interrupting a singer in the warmth of dialogue, in order to wait for a tedious ritornel; or stopping him in the midst of a speech, in order to display the agility of the voice in a large passage. I have not thought it right to pass rapidly over the second part of the air, when it is the most impassioned and important portion of it, in order to repeat the words regularly four times; or to finish where the sense is not complete, in

* This translation is copied from that in Hogarth's Musical Drama

order to give the singer the opportunity of showing that he can vary a passage in several ways according to his own fancy. In short, I have endeavored to reform those abuses, against which good sense and good taste have long exclaimed in vain.

"I have considered that the overture should make the audience aware of the character and subject of the piece; that the instrumental accompaniment should be regulated by the interest of the drama, and ought not to leave a void in the dialogue between the recitative and air; that it should not break into the sense and connection of a period, nor interrupt the warmth and energy of the action. It was also my opinion, that the chief care of a dramatic composer should be to aim at simplicity. I have accordingly avoided making a parade of difficulties at the expense of perspicuity; and I have attached no value to the discovery of novelty, unless it arose naturally from the situation of the character and the expression of the poetry: nor is there any rule of composition which I have not been willing to sacrifice to the production of a good effect.

"These are my principles. Fortunately, the poem has wonderfully favored my views. The celebrated author, having conceived his own plan of the lyric drama, in place of flowery descriptions, useless compositions, cold and sententious morality, has substituted strong passions, interesting situations, the language of the heart, and variety of action. The success of the piece has justified my ideas; and the universal approbation of so enlightened a city has proved to me that simplicity and truth are the greatest principles of the beautiful in the productions of the fine arts."

But composers were slow to recognize and adopt Gluck's principles. It seems even that there were two parties at the Austrian capital,— those who adhered to the ancient form of musical drama, headed by Metastasio and Hasse; and those who represented the new school, headed by Gluck and Calzabigi. Gluck himself thought it necessary to defend his new principles, in regard to a true musical drama, against the objections of the critics; for in the dedicatory epistle published with the opera "Paride ed Elena," complaining at the same time of the indifference with which composers received his new endeavors, he says, "I determined to publish the music of 'Alceste,' simply in the hope that it might find imitators. I ventured to flatter myself, that, in following the path I have already opened, composers would have endeavored to put an end to the abuses introduced into the Italian theatre, and by which it is dishonored;

but I grieve to confess, that, hitherto, my endeavors have been in vain. The half-learned, the pretenders to taste, unhappily too numerous a class, and in all ages a thousand times more injurious to the progress of the fine arts than those who are entirely ignorant, have combined against a method, which, in establishing itself, destroyed their pretentions.

"It was thought that judgment might be pronounced upon 'Alceste,' after irregular, ill-directed, and worse-executed rehearsals. The effect which this opera would produce in a theatre was calculated in an apartment with the same sagacity with which some Grecian critics pretended to judge, at the distance of a few feet, of the effect of statues to be placed on lofty columns. One of these nice amateurs, who has transferred his whole soul to his ears, will find an air too hard, a passage too much marked, or not sufficiently prepared, without dreaming that, in that particular situation, this air and passage are the height of expression, and produce the happiest contrast. A pedantic harmonist will remark an ingenious negligence or a deficiency in strictness, and will hasten to denounce them as unpardonable violations of the mysteries of harmony; and, forthwith, a chorus of voices will join in condemning the music as rude, barbarous, and extravagant."

Though Gluck began to introduce his reforms while composing for the stage of the German capital, yet Germany was not prepared to offer an advantageous field for the realization of his principles, carried to their last consequences; and it is a question, whether he ever could have pursued his plans, had he not found in the individuality and characteristics of a foreign people (the French) those qualities and peculiarities of musical culture which proved favorable to his own aims and ideas of what the musical drama should be. The Bailly *du Rollet*, an attaché of the French embassy at Vienna, passionately fond of poetry and music, and an admirer of Gluck's, pointed out to the composer the stage of Paris as the only place, where, under existing circumstances, success was possible. Monsieur du Rollet proposed Racine's favorite drama, "Iphigenia in Aulis," for their first trial, to be brought out on the Paris stage: he was willing to submit Racine's drama to those modifications required by the musical composer. Gluck, of course, hesitated not a moment to accept du Rollet's propositions; and, with the energy and enthusiasm of a convinced reformer, he threw his whole mind into the balance, in order to make "Iphigenia" acceptable to the taste of his future Paris audience, and at the same time to put forth his new ideas in the most perfect form. But, before we accompany Gluck to the French capital, I will briefly survey the situation of the field Gluck was on the point of entering.

I have already spoken of the labors of Lully and Rameau, and the importance their works assumed in the history of the musical drama. When Gluck's "Iphigenia in Aulis" appeared, Paris was divided into two camps, the "Bouffonists," and the "Anti-Bouffonists." The first were the champions of the Italian opera, in whose ranks we see such writers as Rousseau, and the German Baron von Grimm, who asserted, in elaborate essays, that the French language was not fit to be set to music, and ridiculed the representations of French opera with the most cutting sarcasm. The "Anti-Bouffonists" were represented by those who swore by Lully and Rameau. French composers, such as Dauvergne and Mondonville, strove individually to cultivate the forms of the opera in the sense of Rameau; or like Duny, Philidor, and Gretry, to realize, in their operas, a fusion of the Italian and the French elements. This was the case with the French opera when Gluck engaged in it. The realism of one-sided musical expression had here, as in Italy, come to such a pass that interest in the poem was almost lost sight of. The text-books were mere consoles for musicians to display their pictures upon. The poet's office was limited to that of reproducing well-known situations, with a few variations, adapted to the prevailing taste. Rousseau* falsely accused the French language of causing this tiresome monotony, when it should properly have been laid to the account of a one-sided artistic direction. The genius of the French language opposes as much resistance to the melodic breadth of ornamental song as the Italian tongue is opposed to strong declamation. This misunderstanding between words and music had not escaped the fine observation of Gluck. Avoiding a fruitless reconciliation between them, he took hold of the declamatory principle energetically, and carried his idea out with iron firmness, cutting off the over-luxuriant growth of melody on all sides, regulating the musical expression to the thought and the laws of prosody. To the melodic cut of his arias, he allowed only such liberty as the truth of the dramatic expression demanded; to his chorus, he assigned a broad phrase form, and a sufficient polyphonic treatment. He gave to the recitative its full value; in fact, revealed such a richness of form in the recitative style, heightened by strikingly dramatic instrumentation, that it fully made amends for a somewhat too spare use of melodic charm. He also perfected the overture,

* In his "Lettres sur la Musique française."

placed it in undoubted relationship to the poem, and gave it a peculiarly dramatic stamp. In all these respects, Gluck went further than his French predecessors, and, to a great extent, completed in this the labor of Rameau.

Gluck, with that firmness and impetuosity of character, with that energy and obstinate perseverance, with that enthusiastic faith in his own powers, — qualities so indispensable to an exponent of new and reformatory doctrines, — entered the battle-field with confidence. The 14th of February, 1774, "Iphigenia in Aulis" was performed in Paris. Though the success of the first representation was not a brilliant one, yet the victory was decided; but, at the same time, opposition from both parties, the "Bouffonists" and the "Anti-Bouffonists," was instigated against the new intruder. Gluck's star, however, rose higher and higher. "Orfeo," "Alceste," both re-arranged for the wants of the Paris stage, confirmed his reputation. "Iphigenia in Tauris," and "Armide" followed; and, with every new representation of these works, the supremacy of Gluck's principles was confirmed, though not without a hard final struggle with the Italian opera. The champions of Italian music, alarmed at the progress of Gluck's operas, and anticipating defeat through the very principles of Lully and Rameau, which they so often had ridiculed, and which the genius of Gluck had rehabilitated in a new, more poetical, and more acceptable garb, called to their support that Italian composer of the day, who, with sure success, could alone be opposed to Gluck; *Piccini*, a composer of great merit, and especially endowed with fine melodic talent. He arrived at Paris in 1776. My space will not allow me to enlarge upon all that was done, said, and published by both parties,—the "Gluckists" and "Piccinists"—to sustain their course: suffice it to say here, that party feeling ran high; from the court down to the public in the parterre, the two parties heaped bon-mots, sarcasm, even gross abuse, upon each other, and pamphlets *pro* and *con*, rained on the passive spectators. For illustration's sake, I will mention, that, at the first representation of Piccini's "Roland," the composer, after assisting at the rehearsal, and seeing the animus of the performers, said to Marmontel, his librettist, "Every thing goes wrong." And in the evening, when he started to be present at the performance, he consoled his alarmed friends,—"Come, my children," he said, "this is unreasonable: we are living with the politest and kindest nation of Europe. If they do not like me as a musician, they will, at all events, respect me as a man and a stranger." Though Piccini succeeded temporarily, time has since adjusted all those party differences. Piccini's works are forgotten; while Gluck's are still performed, and attract the admiration of the connoisseur.

Gluck died in Vienna, Nov. 15, 1787.

FIFTH LECTURE.

The Development of Instrumental Music from the Sixteenth Century to Haydn.

SONG, the earliest emanation of the world of feelings and emotions within the soul, was first uttered by that musical organ which is identical with man's existence, the human voice. The improvement of this organ through careful culture, until it became a highly artistic instrument, was, as far as we know, the first endeavor of civilized man; and, as man's highest natural inclination is to devote his finest gifts to the glory of the Creator, song became, at an early period of human culture, the ornament of all temple service. It was, however, as I have already shown in my previous lectures, in the bosom of the Church that song first created its own artistic forms, in conformity with the sacred office it had to fill. Though old Greek, Roman, and Hebrew authors are lavish in their praise of the astonishing effects of instrumental music, as used in their several temple services, yet it was not till the latter part of the sixteenth century that a really artistic signification was attached to the cultivation of instrumental music. To judge from the construction and nature of the sacred instruments known to the old Greeks, Hebrews, and Romans, these instruments, for the most part, must have been only used for dynamic effects, to enliven and mark the rhythm of the sacred dances and the triumphal marches, or to regulate, in Greek tragedy, the motion of the chorus. The Christians, though at first averse to the music and musical instruments of the heathens, accepted many of the heathen customs by degrees, as also their instruments; for we know, that, even in some churches of the Orient, instrumental music was finally introduced. The different Celtic races also possessed several kinds of musical instruments, such as the Irish harp, and Crowth, or Rotta, a kind of violin in a very primitive state of construction. The German races, no doubt, also brought with them, on their migration to the southern provinces of Europe, divers types of musical instruments, as used by them to accompany their songs and dances; but it was not until the general introduction of harmony, that men, gifted with musical talent, began, by means of new inventions, to perfect the mechanism of different instruments, and were thus enabled to exploit the resources of these instruments for more artistic purposes. Instrumental music, if not destined for church service, was, however, for a long time despised by professional composers: its crude execution was therefore left entirely to uneducated men and women. In some parts of Germany and France, these musicians formed regular corporations: they had their own constitution, which was sometimes sanctioned by the king or the count in whose domains they resided. They consequently enjoyed the exclusive privilege of playing at, and also furnishing music for, the different festivities of the inhabitants of cities and villages. The head of the corporation was called the "King of the Pipers," or the "King of the Fiddlers." Thus, in the middle ages, we have the jongleurs and minstrels, — a class of people very little respected, but welcomed everywhere for their music, their songs, and their jests. The pieces they played were no doubt folk-songs in the different dance forms, adapted to the instruments then in use. The music-books of the sixteenth century contain many pieces to be played as dances; such as the passamezzo, the gaillard, the saltarello, the pavane, the imperial, the bransle, &c.; but these dances were all tunes of favorite folk-songs: they were arranged for the organ, the harpsichord, the lute, the guitar, the viols, and other instruments. The manner of expressing, by means of alphabetic letters, the sounds given by the strings or stops of the different instruments was called *tabulatura*, or *tablature:* it is what we to-day denominate *score.*

Although a great number of various musical instruments were already known, and in use, in the sixteenth century, yet instrumental music made but slow progress; while vocal music had already attained at this time, a high degree of perfection. It is true, that, though acquainted with the principal instruments then in practice, composers directed all their attention to the composition of choral music. If, besides dance music, other pieces of a more serious character were to be played, the musicians selected such as were written in polyphonic style, like motets, madrigals, and also folk-songs, set in contrapuntal manner. Thus, we often read on the title-pages of the publications of motets, madrigals, and other secular songs, — that they may be sung and also played on different instruments, — *da cantare e sonare.* This proves that instrumental music, in its forms as independent of choral or vocal music, is entirely a modern art, not over two hundred years old. The direction which musical art takes in our time is vastly different from that which it followed in the sixteenth century. Then the cultivation of vocal music was the chief object of composers: to-day, and principally since the appearance of the three great Vienna masters, Haydn, Mozart, and Beethoven, instrumental music has obtained the ascendency.

Vocal and instrumental music aim at the same æsthetical purpose: they are both the instrumentalities of expressing, by means of adequate ideal artistic forms, those feelings, those emotions of joy and sorrow, which move man's soul. Vocal music found its first and gradual perfection in connection with poetry: the musical imagination of man was thus assisted by the support of decidedly-expressed sentiments. In the course of time, and by means of long experience, a vocabulary established itself of fixed melodious forms, corresponding with those of mere language, for the expression of man's ideal inner life. Only then, when this important æsthetical ground was gained, was it possible for purely instrumental music to create its own peculiar forms on the basis of those vocal ones. In adapting and arranging vocal pieces for their instruments, musicians already strove, and were also in many cases forced, to observe as much as possible the peculiar construction which influenced the technical treatment of these instruments. In running through the score of a motet or a madrigal, as originally composed for voices and then arranged for instruments, the difference is apparent. The facility of sustaining, as much as the composer's idea required it, the various tones which composed a melody,—a peculiarity of the human voice,—was out of the question, when these same melodies had to be played on the lute, the harpsichord, or the viols, then the favorite instruments. Rhythm and motion being the predominant character of these instruments, the players supplied the want of long-sustained notes by varying the principal tones of the melody. This manner of arranging and varying consisted of different ornaments, such as trills, turns, passages, tremolos, or by diminishing a long note into a corresponding number of notes of smaller value. This way of varying a melody, or note-splitting, was also called diminution, or coloring; hence, the expression, "coloratura," as applied to vocal execution. The diminution, or coloring, was, however, diligently exercised by the human voice; and the pieces for the organ of this period prove that the organists also delighted in this manner of playing. Vincenzo Galilei, who played such a conspicuous part in the invention of the opera, complains of these musical "embroiderers" of his time, who, by their changes and divisions, so disguised every melody that it was no longer recognizable, "but resembled the representations of the first painters in oil, which required the names to be written under them for the convenience of the spectator, who, without such assistance, would have been unable to distinguish a rose from a lily, a sparrow from a linnet, a lobster from a trout." But, nevertheless, the peculiar material out of which instrumental music was to build up its forms, was thus gradually gained.

There is no time here to trace the origin, and follow up the gradual perfection, of every instrument I shall mention in this lecture. I will start from that point where each relative instrument was already made fit to serve some artistic purpose.

The instrument, which, among others, seems to have received the first careful attention of composers, was the organ. Its gradual perfection went hand in hand with that of counterpoint; and history tells of a great organist, Francesco Landino, who lived in the fourteenth century, in Venice; but as none of his compositions for the organ have come down to us, they must have been, to judge from the awkward state of the key-board of the organ, just as awkward and crude efforts. Of the so-much praised organists, Bernhard, the German (to whom the invention of the pedal is probably wrongly attributed), and Antonio Scarcialupi, who lived in the fifteenth century in Italy, we do not know much more.

Of greater importance for us is *Conrad Paumann* of Nuremberg, who also lived in the fifteenth century. Though born blind, he had made himself master of most of the instruments in use at his time. His pieces for the organ, of which quite a number still exist, are written in a very fluent counterpoint, in two and three parts. These pieces also give evidence of the advanced state of contrapuntal art at this epoch in Germany, being the oldest known specimens of pieces for keyed instruments: they also show, that there already existed a marked difference between the manner of "coloring" for the voice and that practised on instruments. Here are two of Paumann's pieces, as deciphered by Henry Bellermann.

18.

19.

The names of quite a number of organists, contemporaries of Paumann, and who were then more or less celebrated, have been preserved; which is also a proof that the art of master Conrad was already generally cultivated through Germany. I will mention Paul Hofhaimer, Wilhelm Legrant, Paumgartner, George von Puttenberg: other German masters who lived at a later period were Arnold Schlick, Jacob Buus, Ammerbach, Bernhard Schmid, and Jacob Paix. These masters, though their compositions present for the most part nothing but the before-mentioned art of varying or splitting notes, laid the first foundation of that great school of German organists of which J. S. Bach forms the culminating point.

The religious and social life of the people being in the fourteenth, fifteenth, and sixteenth centuries so intimately connected, the forms of musical art admitted by the Church, also exercised their influence over those destined for amusement in the home circle; and thus the organ was to be found in the house of the private citizen as well as in the church. The art of organ-playing, and the cultivation of instrumental music in general, was, of course, diligently pursued by the great masters of counterpoint, — the Netherlanders. The most celebrated among them seems to have been *John Peter Sweling*, organist in Amsterdam, born in 1540 + 1622. His reputation was so great, that from all parts of Germany young organists came to profit by his lessons. He was called in Hamburg the "organist's manufacturer." Several great masters, distinguished as composers of fine choral works, as well as skilled organists, lived in Italy at this epoch. I will mention *Girolamo Parabosco*, *Andrea*, and *Giovanni Gabrieli*, *Merula*, *Frescobaldi* (called the father of true organ-playing), and *Pasquini*. All these masters contributed in a considerable degree to the perfection of the forms of organ music, as also of instrumental music in general; and many of their pieces, such as toccatas and fugues, yet possess merit. The toccata seems to have received the greatest attention from these masters. Its form, no doubt, has grown up with those short pieces, at first of no distinct form, — short improvisations, as I should call them, — such as *fantasies*, *ricercari*, *capricci*, *contrapunti*, *introduzioni*, *canzone*, which were played before a fugue or a motet; or, as an old author says, "before the organist or cembalist plays a fugue or a motet, he will strike simply, and in a plain manner, a few chords and passages." The toccata has always preserved the style of free improvisation. The more developed melodious form gives place in it to motivos of lively passages and broken chords, — arpeggios; and though worked up with all the art of counterpoint (as are those of J. S. Bach), liveliness and spirited motion, reminding us of instantaneous improvisation and inspiration, are its distinguishing features. The old masters must have used the above-mentioned expressions, *fantasia*, *ricercare*, &c., which invariably convey to our mind a piece in this or that distinct form, without attaching to them as much difference of meaning as we do; at least, to judge from the construction of their pieces, composed for the organ or the harpsichord. *Ricercare*, or *ricercata*, for instance, means a master fugue, — an art fugue; that is to say, a fugue in which all intricacies of double counterpoint and the canon find a place: while, with those old organists, it meant simply a piece in the style of a fantasie or extemporization.

The keyed instruments in use in the sixteenth century, and out of which our square, upright, and grand piano-fortes sprung, were the virginal, the spinet, the clavichord, and the harpsichord. Instead of the hammer which strikes the strings in our modern piano-forte, the key in those old instruments raised little wooden jacks, furnished with a crow-quill, or with a piece of brass or steel, which struck the wires. The sound which these instruments produced, though thin, was yet free and clear: altogether, it had something dreamy and romantic about it; and, when played softly, a good deal of the æolian harp. The virginal, "the instrument for the ladies," as an old writer calls it, was much in favor at the court of Queen Elizabeth of England. The queen herself seems to have been a good performer on this instrument. She was very desirous of gaining supremacy as a virginal player over Queen Mary of Scotland, and practised diligently with that object. Sir James Melvil tells us, that one day, while at the queen's court, Lord Hursden drew him up to a quiet gallery, where he might hear the queen play upon the virginal. "After I had harkened a while," he says, "I took by the tapestry that hung before the door of the chamber, and, seeing her back was toward the door, I entered within the chamber, and stood a pretty space, hearing her play excellently well; but she left immediately, so soon as she turned about and saw me. She appeared to be surprised to see me, and came forward, seeming to strike me with her hand, alleging, she used not to play before men, but when she was solitary, to shun melancholy. She inquired whether my queen (Queen Mary) or she played best. In that, I found myself obliged to give her the praise." A volume of pieces called "Queen Elizabeth's virginal book" is still preserved. The compositions, consisting of preludes, dance tunes, and variations on popular songs, were written by Tallis, Bird, Farnaby, and Dr. Bull. Orlando Gibbons also composed a considerable number of pieces for the virginal and the organ. To judge from these pieces, which are most of them very dry exercises, all these English composers must have already possessed remarkable facility in mastering, on the virginal, the harpsichord, and the organ, all sorts of difficulties; and Dr. John Bull especially, through his extensive powers, must have been a kind of Thalberg at this early epoch of instrumental music.

One of the most favorite instruments of all nations, particularly during the sixteenth and seventeenth centuries, was the *lute*. Though it is long out of practice, and forgotten, our poets, perhaps for the sake of its euphonious name, still dream of its romantic qualities. I will, therefore, give a somewhat detailed explanation and account of the nature of this instrument. The shape of the body of the lute was not unlike that of a turtle. Attached to it was a long neck, inlaid with nine frets, which marked the intervals, and over which the strings ran: at the extremity of the neck was attached the head, or the cross into which the screws, destined to tune the strings, were fixed. The instrument was not unlike the guitar, but it had more strings,—from eight to twenty-four. I extract from Mace's "Musik's Monuments" the following passage, which will convey to you an idea of the manner in which it was played. Mace was a passionate lover of the lute, and placed it above all other instruments. "Now, as to this order," he says, "first set yourself down against a table, in as becoming a posture as you would choose to do for your best reputation. Sit upright and straight; then take up your lute, holding it in a slanting position, the head erected against your left shoulder and ear. Lay your left hand down upon a table, and your right arm over the lute, so that you may set your little finger down upon the body of the lute, just under the bridge, against the treble or second string, and then keep your lute stiff, and strongly set, with its lower edge against the table edge; and so, holding it firmly, cause it to stand steady and strong, so that a bystander cannot easily draw it from you. This is the most becoming, steady, and beneficial posture." The instrument must have been of a very fragile construction; for, says our old author, "You must know that once in a year or two, if you have not very good luck, you will be constrained to have its body taken off: because, being so very thin, and only supported with six or seven small weak bars, and by the constant stretch of the strings (which is a great strength), the body will often sink in; and then your lute will jar, and grow unpleasant." Mattheson, the contemporary of Handel, and a prolific writer on musical subjects, did not think very favorably of the lute. "The flattering lute," he says (in his 'Neu-eroeffnetes Orchester'), "has really more partisans than it deserves. The insinuating sound of this deceiving instrument always promises more than it can keep; and, before one knows the strong and weak points of a lute, one is inclined to think that there cannot exist in this world any thing more charming: but, after a closer acquaintance with this siren among instruments, one will soon be convinced of its great defects, one of which is the everlasting tuning; for, if a lute-player reaches the age of eighty, he assuredly has spent sixty years of his life in tuning. In fact, it has been said, that it costs the same money to keep a lute in Paris as a horse." This instrument, in spite of its defects, was held in great favor by amateurs and musicians until the latter part of the last century, when it disappeared entirely. The instrument *theorbe* is a large lute.

Though it was already the custom, in the sixteenth century, to unite the sound of different musical instruments with that of the human voice, in order to perform the various vocal pieces for the church, as well as in private chapels of kings and princes, and also to increase the resonance and to enrich the body of the sound, yet it was not until the middle of the seventeenth century that the accompanying of purely instrumental music received more attention, and became of more importance. The different instruments in use at this epoch were only added at first to double the vocal parts. There were then no extra parts written for the instrumental performers: they transposed and arranged the vocal parts for their instruments in the best way they could. To judge from the character of these instruments and the powers of the performers, such a performance must have been a curious cacophony. If a singer desired to sing alone, and as melodious pieces for one voice were not yet composed, he would choose a piece written in a contrapuntal style, sing the upper part as the air, and play, on a guitar or a lute, the other parts as an accompaniment. With the invention of the musical drama, the opera, and its formal perfection, instrumental music began to emancipate itself from the fetters of custom, as a mere double of the original vocal parts. In the recitative and the airs, it was soon found necessary to sustain the singer through a careful and direct harmonic accompaniment; while, at the same time, it was of the greatest consequence not to interfere with the freedom of his dramatic action. Thus, instruction to this effect had to be given by the composer; and consequently separate and explicit parts had also to be written for the accompanying instrumentalists. Short pieces, called symphonies, were used to introduce the different scenes; and similar pieces, called ritornellos, were played between or at the close of the parts. These were not pieces of a fixed form, but merely improvisations. Favorite dance tunes were also frequently used for the same purpose.

The instruments which are said to have composed the orchestra of the first opera, the "Euridice" by Rinuccini, were a harpsichord, a large guitar, a viol, a large lute, and flutes. Though some modern authors do not mention any other instruments used in this first opera, it is very probable, that, to give more eclat to the performance of his work, which was played on such a great occasion as the marriage of the King of France with a daughter of the house of Medicis, Rinuccini used all the instrumental resources then at his disposal; for we find that the number of instruments used at some previous festivities in Florence was very considerable. Forty different ones are mentioned, which had to play the accompaniments and the ritornellos on a grand occasion in 1565. Here is the longest instrumental piece, which introduces a scene in Rinuccini's "Euridice:" it is for three flutes, and consists of fourteen bars.

20.

To the masters of the Venetian school of music, and foremost among them to *Giovanni Gabrieli* * and *Claudio Monteverde*, belongs most of

* K. von Winterfeld: Johannes Gabrieli und sein Zeitalter.

the credit of having in a certain degree created new and independent forms for instrumental music, and also of having given a truer and, at the same time, a more effective style of instrumental accompaniment. Thus the line of demarcation between choral and instrumental music began to be more distinct; yet each of them lent to each other more support, more effective meaning. In Monteverde's operas, we already find quite a number of independent instrumental pieces, such as symphonies, ritornellos, toccatas, romanescas, maurescas, ricercares. The desire of employing different instrumental means for the characteristic and dramatic coloring of the various scenic situations is apparent in all his dramatic compositions, particularly in the battle-scene between Tancred and Clorinda, from Tasso's "Jerusalem Delivered," performed in 1624. It is the scene which describes the encounter of Tancred with Clorinda, whom Tancred meets in the night, and, armed as she is, believes her to be one of the heathen warriors. The composer, by means of four string instruments (three violas, and a double bass), unfolds before our mind a picture which reflects, with great dramatic truth and life, the inner, passionate emotions of the two eager combatants, and also the spirited exciting combat. The words of the poet, sung in recitative style, describe this. A passage in triple time imitates and represents the hasty and impetuous approach of the horses. Scales, played in alternate and quick

21. a.

succession, open the duel, and in the hottest of the fight break free from control, and dissolve in chords played with great rapidity in the manner

b.

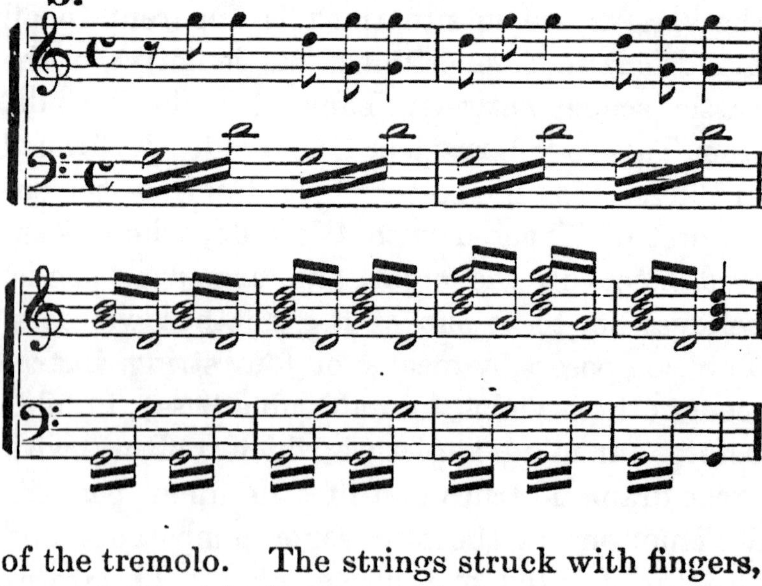

of the tremolo. The strings struck with fingers, instead of with the bow, *pizzicato* as we call it to-day, produce chords that imitate the noise of the warriors' helmets striking against each other

c.

Passages of syncopated notes give an ingenious picture of the close struggle of the combatants.

d.

In their eager desire for victory, they grasp, they avoid, they deceive each other. At last, when

e.

Clorinda is wounded by a stroke from Tancred's sword, and they interrupt the fight, the major key changes into a minor. Fatigued, exhausted, lifting the helmet of his wounded and dying supposed enemy, Tancred recognizes Clorinda, the woman he loves so much. I give you

a detailed description of this remarkable effort of descriptive dramatic music, as it is one of the most striking documents of musical art at this early epoch. With a keen sense and great ingenuity, Monteverde here for the first time used instrumental effects entirely different from the vocal ones, and opened the road to his successors. "It is well to know," he says, "that I am the author of the invention and the first use of this manner of writing, so necessary in musical dramatic art; for, without its knowledge, musical art was incomplete, having thus far only expressed the quiet and the soft." When first performed, the instrumentalists thought it

14

ridiculous to repeat the same note sixteen times (tremolando); but Monteverde, sure of his design, and convinced of the dramatic truth of his intentions, removed their objections; while, at the same time, he taught them how to execute the new difficulties: and the effect of the performance of this scene was astonishing, overwhelming. He thus at once surpassed all his predecessors in their efforts to produce dramatic music.

Though this manner of tone painting — that is, expressing and representing to the mind, by means of instrumental effects and combinations, the different emotions and situations the poem thus describes — is in a certain degree a new invention attributed to Monteverde, yet, in fact, it is only a transposition, for the peculiar mechanism of instruments, of what had already been done by Monteverde himself, and by other masters who lived before and with him, in some of their madrigals and chansons. I take, for instance, "La Battaglia Taliana," a battle-piece by Matthew le Maistre, from the year 1552, and composed for four voices. It is an extremely lively, spirited, and ingenious tone-picture: the sound of the trumpet, the booming of the cannon, the rattling of musketry, the gallop of the horses, and all the excitement of a lively contest, are imitated very faithfully by means of vocal combinations and characteristic syllables and words. Monteverde, endowed with great penetration and practical sense, no doubt understood at once with what great advantage and effect, instruments, in preference to voices, may be used in similar forms, leaving to each one of them its own peculiarity, but, when combined, drawing out of them such resources as render his tone-picture more complete, more effective. In this sense, he may be regarded, and perhaps with more reason than any other of his contemporaries, as the real creator of modern dramatic and instrumental music.

With the gradual introduction of the dramatic element, the formal construction of musical art changed entirely. The distinguishing characteristics of the ecclesiastical keys are, a strict use of diatonic melodic forms, and the observance of the relative position of the semi-tone (mi fa) in all the scales or modes (see these scales in the first lecture). Through this, each one of the modes is subjected to a peculiar harmonic treatment, and different closing formulas (cadenzas). The difference between the various keys is thus more marked than that between our modern major and minor keys, and their transposition to other degrees. This led the old writers to attribute to every one of the ecclesiastical keys the power of individual expression and effect; but, like some of our modern theorists, who vainly endeavor to explain, in a similar way, the character of our major and minor keys, these old authors do not at all agree as to the nature of feeling expressed by each ecclesiastical key. Towards the middle of the sixteenth century, however, freer rules in the practice of the old modes began to be made use of; adherence to their purely diatonic character became gradually less strict. Through the efforts of the madrigal composers, and especially the masters of the Venetian school, the chromatic element, degree by degree, modified the austerity of the diatonic character of the ecclesiastical keys: for, in the madrigal, composers moved more independently in formal construction; and, by means of the harmonic innovations, so freely introduced in the madrigal, the rigid and long-sanctioned ecclesiastical forms of the old mass began, in the course of time, to be entirely abandoned. Space will not allow me to enter into more detail on the construction of the ecclesiastical keys. For a closer study, consult J. J. Fux's "Gradus ad Parnassum" (1725, Vienna), and Padre Martini's "Esemplare osia Saggio fondamentale pratico di Contrappunto" (1774–75, 2 vols. Bologna). But, above all, I would refer to the actual musical works of the old church composers.

Monteverde was one of the first masters

(perhaps the first) who freely introduced the chord of the dominant seventh, in our modern sense; through this he contributed, more than any other composer, to the overthrow of the ecclesiastical keys, and the substitution instead, of our modern tonalities, governed by the dominant seventh, and the tonic. These modes lie at the sources of nearly all folk-songs and dance-tunes. Instrumental music, in a great degree founded on these popular forms, thus created its own forms and tonal modes. With the supremacy of the major and minor modes, the material of our modern musical art began to develop itself with more freedom, with more fluency, rendering it at the same time more pliable to the wants and requirements of the dramatic and instrumental composer.

Monteverde's successors, such as Carissimi, Cesti, Scarlatti, took up the work of perfecting dramatic music, as well as of using the instruments with more refinement and effect. The noisy wind instruments, forever out of tune (their construction having not yet attained such a high degree of perfection as in our modern times), disappear entirely from the orchestra, or are employed with more discretion. The accompaniment is limited to string instruments, the harpsichord, and the lute or theorbe In the church, instead of trombones, cornetti, and trumpets, string instruments are frequently united with the organ. Thus more contrast and artistic effect was gained in the performance of cantatas, masses, and oratorios.

With the perfection of construction in the family of string instruments, such as violins, violas, violoncellos, and double basses, by the celebrated violin-makers, Amati, Guarneri, Stradivari, Stainer, &c., some of whom were already celebrated at the end of the sixteenth century, the art of violin-playing was first brought in Italy to that high degree of execution and artistic performance, in which the Italian virtuosi soon rivalled the great singers. The musician, who through his mastery as a performer on the violin, and also through the fine and noble compositions which he wrote and published for this instrument, contributed more than any other of his contemporaries towards the development of our modern chamber music, was *Arcangelo Corelli*, born in 1653, at Fusignano, near Bologna. Corelli, when scarcely yet known, made a tour through Germany, where he played at some princely courts with great applause and distinction. After a few years of residence in that country, and principally at Munich, he went back to Italy, and made Rome his permanent home. Corelli, as a violin-player, is said to have distinguishe l himself through a round, pure, and very refined tone; and, though his technical skill and execution of great difficulties were surpassed by many good orchestral leaders of his time, yet, through his noble, exquisite, and truthful expression, and his classic compositions he surpassed them all. As such, he is with right considered the father of violin-playing. Corelli was a very modest and amiable artist, but a very sensitive one. Handel, while in Rome, had one of his overtures performed there. Corelli played the first violin in the orchestra on this occasion, and according to his own style, which was very refined, but full of sentiment, missed the spirited, grand idea of the composer. Handel, losing all patience, took in his customary brusque way Corelli's violin, in order to show him how he meant to have his work played. "But, my dear Saxon," said Corelli very gently, "your overture is written in the French style, which I do not understand." Corelli had already experienced the fickleness of the public, which very often condemns, and forgets next morning the artist it vociferously applauded the evening before. While on a short visit to Naples, a virtuoso on the hautboy, and another on the violin, — both much inferior to him, — won the admiration and the applause of the Romans; thus, when back in Rome, he thought himself forgotten. This caused him so much chagrin, tha,, it is said to have shortened his days He died in 1712. Corelli published a great many works for string instruments, with accompaniment of a figured bass. Other great violin-players at this epoch were *Geminiani*, a pupil of Corelli, *Vivaldi*, *Veraccini*, and, above all, *Giuseppe Tartini*, born at Istria, in 1692. To judge from Tartini's compositions for the violin, he must have possessed an extraordinary mastery over his instrument: they are full of all sorts of difficult passages, trills, double-trills, and skips. His playing was distinguished by a full, round, and pure tone; by great elegance, but a free, yet energetic bowing. Tartini's early life was full of romance. As a youth, his parents wished him to enter a Franciscan convent; but he had no inclination for such a secluded life. He afterwards frequented the University of Padua, in order to study law. Endowed with rare intelligence and great natural facility, he mastered his studies with ease; and, besides his continual cultivation of the violin, he found ample time to devote to the art of fencing, which he loved passionately. Having become very expert in the handling of the sword, and being also confident of his own ability, his quarrelsome temper induced him to fight one duel after the other: he thus neglected his studies, and even entertained the idea of establishing himself in

Paris, as a fencing-master. He would have probably thus been lost to musical art, of which he was destined to be in more than one respect a most worthy representative; but, having fallen in love with a young lady of Padua, the niece of Cardinal Cornaro, he married her secretly. This secret union having become publicly known, his parents, irritated at his ill-conduct, refused him all further subsidies; and the cardinal, enraged at his boldness, set the police to watch him. Tartini fled towards Rome. On his way to that city, he met a priest, a near relation of his, who, taking pity on his reduced situation, invited him to his own convent in the town of Assisa. At this convent our artist hid for two years; even his young wife did not know what had become of him. In this solitude, and much influenced also by the kindness and the piety of the monks of the convent, he devoted all his time to the study of music, especially violin-playing; one of the monks, being an accomplished musician, assisted him much in his studies. After a secret sojourn of two years in the convent, he was discovered by one of his own townsmen, when playing in the church of the convent at some festivity. The cardinal having meanwhile softened down towards him, he was able to return to his family, — a better and wiser man. He afterwards became chapel-master at the principal church in Padua. He wrote and published a great many compositions of classic value for string instruments, endeavored to establish a new system of harmony, founded a music school at Padua, and formed a great many excellent pupils. I will here only mention the distinguished *Nardini*. Tartini was often called by the Italians, *Il Maestro delle nazioni.* His sonata, "The Devil's Trill," is well known; the circumstance that gave existence as well as its title to this remarkable composition is less so. Tartini writes, "One night, in 1713, I dreamed that I had made a compact with the Devil, who had entered my service: every thing succeeded according to my wishes; my desires were always forseen, and exceeded even, by the anxiety of my servant. I fancied that I gave him my violin to play some airs to me; but I was greatly surprised when I heard so beautiful, so original a sonata, executed with such superior intelligence, that I had never even imagined any thing that could be placed in comparison with it. In breathless astonishment and delight, I awoke, and seized my violin, hoping to recall at least a part of what I had heard; but in vain. The piece I then composed is certainly the best I ever wrote; and I still call it, "The Devil's Sonata:" but it is so far beneath what I heard in my dream, that I would then have broken my violin, and abandoned music forever, had I been in a condition to do so."

Besides the classic schools of violin-playing which the masters already mentioned founded in Italy, the art of harpsichord, or piano-forte playing, could also claim, at this epoch, worthy and ingenious composers and performers. The greatest among all was *Dominico Scarlatti*, born in 1683, and son of the renowned composer Allessandro Scarlatti. Dominico Scarlatti also composed operas and church music, but his greatest importance and merit lay in his compositions for the harpsichord. He designated them sonatas, though they are entirely different from the form which we to-day call sonata: they are pieces in one movement, generally in two parts, built upon very simple, but very spirited, original, and always graceful motivos. They are perfect *genre* pictures, full of elegance, full of poetical contrast, developing, in an ingenious manner, all the resources of his great and perfect mastery over the instrument. Most of these unique pieces sound as fresh and melodious as if they had been composed only yesterday. The following extract may give you an idea of Scarlatti's powers as a harpsichord player: Thomas Roseingrave, himself a performer of some eminence on the harpsichord and organ, while on a visit in Venice, was invited, as a stranger and a virtuoso, to an academia at the house of some nobleman, where, among others, he was requested to sit down to the harpsichord, and favor the company with a toccata, as a specimen *della sua virtù*, of his capacity; and, says he, "finding myself rather better in courage and finger than usual, I exerted myself, and fancied, by the applause I received, that my performance had made some impression on the company." After a cantata had been sung, a young man, dressed in black, and in a black wig, who had stood in one corner of the room, very quiet and attentive while Roseingrave played, being asked to sit down to the harpsichord, began to play. Roseingrave said, when he had heard him, that he thought ten hundred devils had been at the instrument; he never heard such passages of execution and effect before. The performance so far surpassed his own, and every degree of perfection to which he thought it possible he should ever arrive, that, if he had been in sight of any instrument with which to have done the deed, he would have cut off his own fingers. Upon inquiring the name of this extraordinary performer, he was told that it was Dominico Scarlatti.

Other distinguished Italian performers on the harpsichord, and, at the same time, composers of merit for this favorite instrument, at this epoch, were *Durante*, *Paradise*, *Porpora*, *Gasparini*, and *Alberti*.

France at this time also claims having produced clever and original harpsichord and organ players, such as *Chambonnières*, *d'Angelbert*, the *Couperins*, *Marchand*, *Daquin*, *Rameau*. *François Couperin*, called the great, as he was considered the most distinguished master of an illustrious family of musicians, was born at Paris, in 1678. To judge from his compositions, which are elegant, full of spirit and originality, he must have been a very accomplished performer; but his pieces are not seldom so overladen with trills and other ornamental notes, indispensable to an instrumental performer at that time, that the graceful and simple melodies are, so to say, entirely smothered. Couperin also published an instruction-book, "L'art de toucher le Clavecin," which was of great influence on the further development of piano-playing. Couperin died in 1733. His greatest immediate successor was *Jean Philippe Rameau*, born at Dijon, in 1683, distinguished as theorist, opera composer, and performer on the organ and the harpsichord. Rameau's compositions for the harpsichord are, in harmonious treatment, as well as in melodious invention, richer than those of Couperin: they are fresh, original, graceful, and very ingenious in formal construction; some of them are real little gems. Rameau died in 1741, and may be considered as the last great master of a series of fine performers of this old French school of piano and organ playing. The custom of giving to many compositions, and also to different dances, for the harpsichord or piano-forte, characteristic titles, such as "La Rare," "La Favorite," "La Fleurie ou la tendre Nanette," "Le Reveilmatin," "La Fanfarinette," "La Musette," &c., &c., suggesting to our mind certain ideas, intended by the composer to be conveyed through them, is not altogether a modern invention. We find that the above-mentioned French composers, as well as German, English, and Italian instrumentalists of that time, made frequent use of this means; to which, however, it is well not to attach too much importance, as it easily leads us to overrate the insignificant and empty fabrications of mere mechanists, who vainly seek to cover their utter want of inventiveness and necessary knowledge, by high-sounding, suggestive titles. It is much more easy to find a pretty title for a piece than to discover fine and effective melodies.

Of English instrumental composers and harpsichord players at this epoch, I must mention *Lawes*, *Locke*, *Roseingrave*, *Purcell*, and *Dr. Blow*. *Henry Purcell* is the most important among them. Some of his sonatas for string instruments, and a harpsichord, and also some of his pieces in the dance forms of his time, are spirited and full of fancy. He well appreciated the melodious and elegant style which distinguished the compositions of such Italian masters as Carissimi, Cesti, Colonna, Bàssoni, Stradella, and, no doubt, studied their works diligently and beneficially; for, in the preface to his twelve sonatas for two violins, and a bass for the harpsichord or organ, he says, "For its author, he has faithfully endeavored a just imitation of the most famed Italian masters, principally to bring the seriousness and gravity of that sort of music into vogue and reputation among our countrymen, whose humor it is time now should begin to loath the levity and balladry of our neighbors (the French). The attempt he confesses to be bold and daring, there being pens and artists of more eminent abilities, much better qualified for the employment than his or himself, which he well hopes these, his weak endeavors, will in due time provoke and inflame to a more accurate understanding. He is not ashamed to own his unskilfulness in the Italian language; but that is the unhappiness of his education, which cannot justly be counted his fault: however, he thinks he may warrantably affirm, that he is not mistaken in the power of the Italian notes, or elegancy of their compositions."

After the beginning of the seventeenth century, instrumental music made great progress, especially in Germany; and the vast number of distinguished talents who devoted all their energy and attention to this branch of musical art soon assured its supremacy in Germany. The organ and the harpsichord, however, were the instruments first cultivated with the greatest success. Since the organ was to lead, and at the same time to accompany, by means of solemn and noble, but simple harmonies, the sacred song, the chorale of the Protestant congregations, its importance began to be more and more conspicuous, and, as such, necessarily also better understood by organists. The chorale, which grew up and was formed in the bosom of the Protestant church, gained for the Protestant organist the same meaning, the same importance, that the Gregorian chant so justly obtained for the great church composers of the fifteenth and sixteenth centuries: it forms the basis of the German-protestant church music. The German organists, the hereditary and faithful cultivators of that great art, counterpoint, in its broadest sense, employed all their science and knowledge to enrich, by means of artistic and suitable organ-playing, the musical part of the Protestant church service, always making the chorale the ground, the principal theme of their efforts.

But how simple and modest were the positions and the pretensions of these honest old organists! And yet, how deep and truthful are the works which they destined for the adornment of religious service! It must have been only through an exceptional perseverance and application, coupled with great love and veneration for the noble art, that they were able to create such fine and numerous works; for the method of instruction was then yet a complicated one, full of unnecessary difficulties, derived in a great measure from the pedantic mania of surrounding it with puerile mysteries. But such masters as Bach and Handel have proven what a solid foundation of musical education this school of German organists was. The Gregorian chant and the Protestant chorale run like a red thread through the musical part of the church service of the two great religious denominations: these really sacred songs of the two churches are the first impressions which touch the soul of the young Christian on his entrance into the Church, and are, as such, the indestructible echoes of his first sacred associations. As Holy Writ forms the invariable foundation of the religious and moral principles of the true Christian, so the Gregorian chant and the chorale ought to form the ground and invariable theme of the true church composer; and, as long as composers understood and valued this inestimable, noble, and really sacred practice, their works composed for the Church truthfully and appropriately fulfilled their solemn office: these works were thus imbued with the sacred character derived from the themes of the sacred songs: then, necessarily, a distinct line of demarcation was drawn between secular and sacred music. How is it to-day? A glance at the meaningless fabrications, destined for the Church by our would-be church composers, will at once betray to you their profane models. The frivolous, worldly variations, and silly, sentimental organ voluntaries, which greet you at your entrance into sacred places, will tell you the source from which the pliant organist has drawn. It is the fashionable opera of to-day, with its worn-out phrases, that has taken the place of the original sacred songs; it is the empty modern ballad that has supplanted the Gregorian chant and the chorale: and, according to my conviction, only a return to the true source of sacred Christian church music will enable our church composers to resuscitate real church art.

The list of celebrated German organists who lived before and with Bach and Handel is long. I shall only mention *Samuel Scheidt*, *John J. Froberger* (the distinguished pupil of the renowned Frescobaldi), *J. C. Kerl*, *J. Pachebel*,

Buxtehude, *Reinken*, *Zachau* (the master of Handel), *George Muffat*, *Fischer*, *Kuhnau*, the predecessor of Bach at Leipzig (and the first who has written a sonata in which we may trace the first dawn of our present sonata form), and the different able organists of that musical family, of which J. S. Bach was the greatest member, while he was at the same time the greatest of all organists. The vast number of immortal works, in every style, which Bach has left for the organ, will serve as the foundation of all true organ-playing, as they will also remain the lofty study of every earnest, striving organist for all time to come. Handel, great in every art-form known at his time, was not less great as an organist. In his concertos for the organ, he has deposited such a treasure of original and beautiful ideas, that it needs only the loving and aspiring mind of the true artist to bring them to light again. And in what glory do Handel's ideas shine, when truly interpreted! All these organists were also distinguished players on the harpsichord, and industrious composers for that instrument. The favorite form of these old composers and harpsichord players was the *suite;* that is, a succession of several movements or pieces in different forms (lessons, as they were also called by old writers), but usually all in the same key. These movements, like those of our modern sonata, — which, in fact, is the substitute of the old *suite*, — were so arranged, as to present the necessary æsthetical contrasts: they differed in time, motion, and rhythm; yet, being all in the same key, the inner relation was to a certain degree preserved. These movements consisted of pieces in the usual dance forms, such as the Allemande, the Couranto, the Gavotte, the Bourrée, the Passacaglia, the Passepied, the Sarabanda, the Pavane, the Air, the Minuetto, the Gigue, the Chaconne, &c., &c. The Preludium also found a place in the suite. Towards the latter part of the eighteenth century, the suite gave place to the partita, to which our modern sonata finally succeeded. I will give here the meaning which the teachers and composers of the seventeenth and eighteenth centuries attached to the character and effect of the different movements which composed a suite, or a course of lessons for various instruments: this gives us a clear insight into the art-practice of our forefathers.

" *The Prelude* is commonly a piece of confused, wild, shapeless, intricate play (as most use it); in which no perfect form, shape, or uniformity, can be perceived, but a random business, — pattering and groping up and down from one stop or key to another, — and generally so performed as to make trial whether the instrument be well in tune or not." Bach, however, gave to the prelude a more artistic form, full of poetical contents.

The Pavane is a grave and majestic Spanish dance, wherein the dancers turn round, and make a wheel or tail before each other, like that of a peacock; whence its name. It was anciently in great repute, and was danced by gentlemen with cap and sword, by those of the long robe in their gowns, by princes with their mantles, and by ladies with their gowns trailing after them. The time thereof is the slowest and gravest part of instrumental music, generally consisting of three strains.

The Couranto is a piece in triple time, commonly of two strains, and full of sprightfulness and vigor, lively, brisk, and cheerful.

The Minuetto is a composition in triple time, of rather slow and graceful motion. It is said to have been invented at Poitou, in France.

The Sarabanda, probably originally derived from Spain, is of a slow and serious character. It is also in triple time.

"*A Tattle de Moy* is a new-fashioned thing, much like a Saraband, only it has more of conceit and humor in it."

"*Jigs* are light, squibbish things, only fit for fantastical, and easy, light-headed people, and are of any sort of time."

The Gavotte is a dance tune of two strains, in common time. It is sometimes of a brisk and lively nature, and sometimes also of a tender and rather slow movement.

The Chaconne (ciacona) is a composition, the characteristic of which is a ground bass, consisting of four measures of three crotchets each, repeated to continually-varied melodies, called couplets. These varied melodies or couplets, passing and re-passing freely from the major to the relative minor key, from the grave to the gay, from the tender to the lively, — but without changing the motion of the time, — form those interesting contrasts which fetter the attention of the listener. I mention, among others, that wonderful chaconne for violin alone, by J. S Bach.

The Passacaglia, or passecaille, is properly no more than a chaconne. The only difference between them is, that the movement of the passecaille is somewhat graver, the time softer, and the expression less lively.

The term *Allemande* represents two kinds of composition. First, a German national dance written in common time, two crotchets in a measure, and of brisk and lively character Then a grave and slow air or melody of four crotchets in a measure.

The suites of Bach and Handel are such exquisite, fresh, and original compositions, that to ignore them is to deprive one's self of genuine musical enjoyment, — every one of their movements is so characteristic, and betrays in every bar the master-hand that formed them.

The suites of *Gottlieb Muffat*, a pupil of the renowned theorist and composer, J. J. Fux, of Vienna, are also rich in fancy and harmony, and worthy productions for the harpsichord of that time. I must also mention that admirable, well-known classical work of Bach's, — the "Wohltemperirte Clavier," or "Well-tempered Piano-forte," a collection of forty-eight preludes and fugues in all the major and minor keys. So great is the artistic value and the intrinsic merit of this work, that, like a rock, it has withstood for more than a century all the changing phases of taste, influenced by the caprices and fashions of time. Eternal youth and unsurpassed perfection stamp every piece of the collection.

It is curious to observe how long it was before these old harpsichord players learned to use all the five fingers as means of artistic execution in a manner that seems so natural to us. Mattheson, as late as 1735, teaches yet the following fingering.

For the right hand, ascending,

C D E F G A B C D E F G A B C
3 4, 3 4, 3 4, 3 4, 3 4, 3 4, 3 4 5:

descending, C B A G F E D C, &c.
5 4 3, 2 3, 2 3, 2 3, &c

Left hand, ascending, descending:
3 2 1, 2 1, 2 1, 2 1, &c.: 2 3, 2 3, 2 3, 2 3. &c.

Bach was here, as ever, the master, who, through his keen sense and his deep appreciation of the true, brought order and system into the application of the use of the fingers, for more effective execution and artistic rendering of the difficulties of keyed instruments.

The orchestral resources of this epoch, by means of diligent practice on, and continual improvement of, the different instruments, were brought to greater effect, principally through those two admirable masters, Bach and Handel, who left the ineffaceable stamp of their genius on every art-form that their minds took hold of. I need only mention Handel's hautboy concertos, his "Fire Music," and many of his overtures to operas and oratorios; Bach's beautiful violin sonatas, orchestra suites, piano-forte concertos, and other instrumental works. They, and their contemporaries, were acquainted with all instruments, except the clarinet, used in our modern orchestra; though they did not yet employ these instruments as the means of creating such varied, rich, and refined combinations, and brilliant effects as we are accustomed to find in the scores of the masters since Gluck and Haydn. In their great choral works, as well as in their purely instrumental compositions, such as overtures, suites, concertos, the string quartet serves as foundation, and occupies a conspicuous part throughout; bassoons, horns, trumpets, kettle-drums, flutes, and hautboys (of which they used several kinds, the ordinary hautboy, the hautboy d'amore, and da caccia) were added, either to strengthen the sonority of greater choral masses, or, as is often the case, especially in Bach's works, they were made to play an individually important part in the different arias. These masters have, however, proved in many of their works, like Bach in his charming D major suite, that they knew how to create ingenious novel instrumental effects when necessary. But these effects grew out of the great idea which lay at the root of the masters' works; they were not used to hide deficiency of melodious inventiveness under a brilliant and highly-colored instrumentation.

The organ, the harpsichord, and formerly the lute, and the theorbe, were always found in the orchestras of these old masters. The art of playing an accompaniment on these instruments, according to the complicated rules of thorough bass playing, seems to be now almost a lost art; and, with this, the *real* tradition of rendering Handel's, Bach's, and other masters' (their contemporaries) works is in a great measure also lost. We know that Handel in his oratorios, and Bach in his cantatas and passion oratorios, made a conspicuous use of the organ, besides the instrumental means of which I have already spoken. In these works, intended and accepted as ideal forms of Protestant church music, the organ, so intimately connected with the religious traditions of every Christian nation, thus inevitably forms an inseparable part. And in its austere grandeur, varied by the resources of the manifold stops, is it not, when well handled, a worthy and fitting background to such works? Revive the art of true organ-playing, as indicated by Bach, Handel, &c., in their numerous works for this instrument, and a great advance towards the true performance of many of these masters' grand choral compositions will be gained. This, however, would necessitate a deeper knowledge of the old masters' (in most senses, unrivalled) method than is generally found among our organists of to-day, and, with it, more thorough study and experience; formerly, masters like Bach himself, were appointed as judges and critics of the aspirants to responsible positions. These places were not then to be gained through social influence alone, or, as is now too often the case, in a sphere where we least look to find it, — through social hypocrisy and intrigue!

The impulse given to instrumental music, especially through the labors and efforts of Bach and his many distinguished disciples in the north of Germany, and through the influence of the great Italian masters of violin-playing in the south of Germany, was lasting and beneficial to art. Kings and princes, some out of love for music, others for ambition's and fashion's sake, supported costly chapels, where an orchestra, composed of able instrumentalists, was the feature. Talented composers were engaged to provide works exclusively for the wants of the eager orchestras of these princely patrons. Solos, trios, concertos, composed by the best masters for various instruments, excited players to develop their own technical skill, and the qualities of their chosen instruments; in this way, such players sometimes rivalled great singers in execution. Thus instrumental practice gained a prominent place and immense importance in German musical culture; and thus also was that great modern German school of instrumental music prepared, headed by *Haydn*, *Mozart*, and *Beethoven*.